The Legalist

The Legalist

Jack Stewart

New Leaf Press

FIRST EDITION
1989

Cover Art by: Jeff Stewart

 For information write: New Leaf Press, Inc., P.O. Box 311, Green Forest, AR 72638.

Typesetting by: Type-O-Graphics
Springfield, MO

Library of Congress Catalog Number: 89-63070
ISBN: 0-89221-177-6

CONTENTS

All Scripture quotations are taken from the King James Bible unless indicated as below:

(NTME) The New Testament in Modern English by J.B. Phillips; Macmillan Publishing Company, New York.

(LOP) The New Testament In The Lanquage Of The People, Chas. B. Williams; Holman Bible Pub., Nashville.

(TLB) The Living Bible, Kenneth Taylor; Tyndale House Pub., Wheaton, IL.

(NIV) New International Version, Zondervan Corp., Grand Rapids, MI.

(NAS) New American Standard Bible, Lockman Foundation, La Habra, CA.

DEDICATION

To
my lovely
wife Beverly,
a love disciple of
Jesus but not a legalist.

Chapter 1

A DAY IN THE LIFE OF A LEGALIST

A day in the life of a legalist is filled with trying to become and never arriving! He seems not to know that *Christ means the end of the struggle for righteousness-by-the-law for everyone who believes in Him* so he fights bravely and hopelessly on!

Dwelling in a perpetual winterland of barrenness, where the cold blasts of condemnation and despair chill his soul, he rarely sees the sunlight of God's love and acceptance! Clouds of doubt and fear overcast the Father's face, Whom he imagines to be more critical than compassionate, frowning than forgiving.

A legalist's day is usually joyless, lifeless, drab, and bound. He is slave to rules: what to eat, drink, wear, and where or where not to go. His life is nearly unbearable! Vainly thinking that doing will achieve being, he forgets that God says, *"Be ye holy."* Holy living flows out of holy being, but evidently he does not understand, so he strains and struggles to lay hold of a righteousness that is forever beyond his reach!

Bible reading, praying, giving, and witnessing are usually looked upon as obligations rather than joyous opportunities for the building and exercising of his faith. The pharisaical strait jacket he wears fails to make him holy, makes him look like he is, and deprives him of the joy of true holiness!

A day in the life of a legalist? Well, it is usually bleak and troubled, self-righteous, or arrogant: it depends on his stance. Mean or miserable, oppressive or oppressed, he cannot rejoice in a right relationship with God! The unkept vows, neglected duties, and disobeyed commandments afflict his conscience until his kind of 'Christianity' is filled with pain! From such religious slavery he needs to be freed, but until he sees Jesus Christ as the all-sufficient answer to his quest for holiness of heart and life, he will labor in his chains!

The legalist can be saved from his days of defeat and failure: and the Saviour is the One Who died for him on Calvary—He is the Liberator!

Legalism's icy breath destroys the budding flowers of God's grace, and thereby robs its followers of the possibility of the fruit of the Spirit! This humanistic religion, as old as the fall of man, deprives its disciples of fellowship with the Creator, while pretending to urge them on to holiness and victorious living. Thriving on rules rather than relationship, it often cloaks a rebellious spirit with the outer garment of seeming righteousness. But spiritual paupers robed in the royal purple of self-righteousness are paupers still!

The *joy of the Lord* and the *fruits of righteousness, which are by Jesus Christ* are forever out of the reach of those who try to attain them by keeping the Law: *For as many as are of the works of the Law, are under the curse: for it is written: Cursed is every one that continueth not in all things which are written in the book of the Law to do them.* (Gal. 3:10) And yet, multitudes attempt to gain holiness and peace by their own works!

Doing is the fruit of a right relationship with God; it is not the root! And the source of all right doing, is right being. In Psalm 1:3, the words *He shall be like a tree planted by the rivers of water* precedes *and whatsoever he doeth shall prosper.*

Legalism is under the curse! Satanic in origin and devastating in its effects, it dominates great numbers of people with its tyranny. Promising life but ministering death, it substitutes 'rules' for the reality of Christ's transforming love and grace. The counterfeit Christianity that results from this exchange is without life and power. Paul's words to the Galatians—*Christ is become of no effect unto you, whosoever of you are justified by the law, ye are fallen from grace* (Gal. 5:4)—are fitting and deserve to be remembered!

God's grace is the only answer to sin! Sin's dominion over us is broken when we are cleansed by the blood of Jesus and sheltered under the divine favor from the demands of the law. Grace that bestows mercy and law that demands death for every offender are completely opposed—we can't be under both! And, when we, by faith, accept God's gift of righteousness, legal ties are severed, and victory is assured.

Martin Luther once said, "There is something about man that he is even more afraid of grace, than he is of law. He is wary, lest receiving the goodness of God should result in careless, sinful living!" Though God's Word says *we are His workmanship created in Christ Jesus for good works* and reveals that *Jesus [is] the author, and finisher of our faith*, we somehow feel that the salvation God began in us can only be continued by our striving to keep the law!

But struggle is not the way to prevail! *The just shall live by faith* is God's prescription for justification and sanctification and is meant to be the lifestyle for all who would live holy. Furthermore, if *the just shall live by faith, and the law is not of faith* then the just shall not live by the law!

Statements like this scare the legalists, for they do not understand that men of faith achieve righteousness and holiness, while those who go *about to establish their own righteousness* do not!

Chapter 2

THE ROOTS OF LEGALISM

Legalism is the gigantic attempt of the flesh to deal with sin! Though it is as old as Adam and Eve's fig leaves and can be seen throughout human history, it is not of God. Self-deceiving and hypocritically pious, it assumes that sin-polluted man can by strenuous effort live a life of holiness. Its devotional masquerade fools many of its followers. Imagining themselves to be spiritual because of their dedication to rules, they are ignorant of God's righteousness. As a result, they go *about to establish their own righteousness* without submitting *themselves unto the righteousness of God*, not realizing that *Christ is the end of the law for righteousness to every one that believeth*. (Rom. 10:3,4)

And yet, since the fall of Adam, mankind has tried to please an infinitely holy God with his own righteousness. Where did this corrupt concept originate? Our first father practiced it when he tried to cover his nakedness ("the badge of his sinfulness") with hand-sewn fig leaves! That effort to clothe his shame and humiliation could not blot out his guilt or make him fit for the presence of God! It was only when *the LORD God [made] coats of skins and clothed them* that they were properly attired and made ready for His gaze! Blood had to be shed, Jehovah had to act, and man had to receive His provision by grace before it was done. It is the same today.

The sinful flesh of every descendent of Adam is no more capable of dealing with the effects of the fall than he was. And yet, we keep on trying! Of one thing we can be sure: if our righteousness is the fruit of our struggle, it is not *the righteousness of God* for His righteousness is a *gift*. Self-justification is not holiness even if it looks like it!

The roots of legalism are in the fall of man, for his depraved nature ever seeks to prove itself worthy of God's commendation. Fleshly pride will never allow a man to admit, *In me (that is, in my flesh) there dwelleth no good thing,* nor will he confess that his sinful being is *wretched, and miserable, and poor, and blind, and naked,* (apart from the Holy Spirit's bringing him to repentance.)

The great tragedy is religious sinners and born-again saints alike seek to gain their acceptance with God through the works of the flesh! Many Christians buy Satan's lie: "You have to keep by works, what you received by grace!" *Having begun in the Spirit* we now seek to be *made perfect by the flesh,* and so we work, work, work, hoping to rest, not knowing that God would have us rest in Christ and cease from our *own works as God did from His.* We too easily forget that *there remaineth therefore a rest to the people of God* and *we which have believed do enter into rest.* And people who rest in Christ work His work! Dr. A. B. Simpson's song, "Himself" says it well:

> "Once it was my working; His it hence shall be.
> Once I tried to use Him, now He uses me!"

Adam could not cleanse himself, cover himself, or save himself, but God did it all for him when he accepted the divine provision for his shame made possible by the shedding of blood! When we realize that salvation, sanctification, and redemption are God's work for men, we will rest all our hopes on *the Lamb of God that taketh away the sin of the world,* and the fruits of righteousness will flow from our lives!

The roots of legalism are deep, but the revelation of the Son of God will dig them up and cut them out! Though they have been firmly imbedded, the knowledge of who Jesus is and what He has done at Calvary will tear loose their grip on the flesh, and the works of self-righteousness will wither and die!

God's answer to the blight of legalism is the One Who *is able to save completly them that come to God by Him.*

A verse of Scripture, Hebrews 10:14 (TLB), should silence forever those who would work their way through to perfection: *he made forever perfect in the sight of God, all those whom he is making holy.* Perfection in His sight and holiness in the life are God's work for men, not men's work for God!

CAIN

The roots of legalism, though founded in fallen Adam, were deeply imbedded in his son, Cain. Manifesting his unbelief and sinfulness by attempting to worship God his own way, he became an example of all humanistic religionists through the ages. His philosophy that a sinful man could come to the infinitely Holy One on another basis than the shed blood of an acceptable sacrifice was proven false in the dawn of history; and it is still false, for *without the shedding of blood, there is no remission of sin!*

Legalism says there is another way to satisfy God besides faith in the Christ of Calvary! It declares that right relationship can be obtained and holiness maintained by our own works. Nearly forty centuries before the cross, Cain's disdain of a blood sacrifice exhibited the rebellion of works-worship. His attitude prevails today in those who would enter the sheepfold not by the door but by some other way. God's rejection of *Cain...and his offering* stands as a testimony for all time of what He thinks about unbelief, and the works of our hands as a way of finding acceptance with Him.

Since Abel's offering of the firstlings of his flock evidenced his faith, and *faith cometh by hearing, and hearing by the Word of God,* Cain also must have known of the necessity for a blood sacrifice, otherwise, God surely would not have held him responsible. His unacceptable worship, therefore, was the result of his rebellion against God's Word because of his unbelief. He thought he could achieve divine approval another way! The fruit of the ground which he brought was the product of that which was cursed. It was a religion of the flesh!

The church world today has multitudes of 'Cains' trying to achieve right standing with God by their own works of righteousness. But they will fail, for the only righteousness that brings acceptance with the Thrice Holy One is Christ's, and it is given to all who repent and believe the Gospel. All manmade attempts to gain the Divine favor are accursed, for *all our righteousnesses are as filthy rags.* To worship in the spirit of Cain is to be rejected; to live with his attitude is to be defeated!

ISRAEL AND THE COVENANT OF GRACE

The covenant of grace God made with Abram preceded the Law by four hundred and thirty years. It was a compact of promise (not of Law), and promises are for faith, not obedience! One does not believe commandments and obey promises; quite the reverse is true.

God's gracious message to Abraham was not "thou shalt, and shalt not do!" It was rather: *I will make thee exceeding fruitful...I will establish my covenant between me and thee and thy seed after thee...to be a God unto thee...I will give unto thee, and to thy seed after thee...all the land of Canaan for an everlasting possession...I will be their God.* (Gen. 17: 6-8) It was not a revelation of what Abram and his seed were to be and do! No, it was the disclosure of God's purposes in grace toward this man of faith and his descendents.

The Abrahamic covenant was not man's reaching out to God, but God's reaching out to man! It was not the reward for Abraham's obedience nor what he deserved for his righteousness. He had none before *he believed in the LORD: and He counted it to him for righteousness.* (Gen. 15:6)

The testimony of Jehovah through the long history of His redemptive purpose has ever been that of a seeking, saving, sanctifying God! He alone is the One *mighty to save, the redeemer of Israel, the Purifier of the sons of Levi.*

Until the giving of the law at Sinai, Abraham's seed had been under the covenant of grace. The results had been glorious:

Ye have seen what I did unto the Egyptians, and how I bare you on eagle's wings, and brought you unto Myself. Now therefore, if you will obey my voice indeed, and keep my covenant, then shall ye be a peculiar treasure unto Me above all people: for all the earth is mine: And ye shall be unto Me a kingdom of priests, and a holy nation. There are the words which thou shalt speak unto the children of Israel. (Ex. 19:4-6)

This covenant of grace, if followed, would have made the whole nation of Israel a kingdom of priests. Instead, under the law, only one tribe (Levi) was made priests! The compact that would have made Israel a holy nation was exchanged for one that could *never ...make the comers thereunto perfect.*

When this people arrogantly said, *''All that the LORD hath spoken, we will do,''* they failed to take into account who they were: sinners by nature!

When we know *that the Law is not made for a righteous man, but for the lawless, and disobedient, for the ungodly and for sinners, for unholy and profane, for murderers of fathers and murderers of mothers, for manslayers, for whore-mongers, for them that defile themselves with mankind, for menstealers, for liars, for perjured persons, and...any other thing that is contrary to sound doctrine,* (I Tim. 1:9-10) then we can also understand God's giving of the Law to Israel at Sinai was, in effect, acknowledging that they were not righteous and were indeed ungodly, unholy, and profane sinners!

When we realize that *the Law made nothing perfect* and Israel's tarnished history is one of ''the golden calf, the broken tables, the desecrated Sabbath, the despised and neglested ordinances, the stoned messengers, the rejected and crucified Christ, the resisted Spirit,''[1] we are made fully aware of *what the Law could not do, in that it was weak through the flesh.* (Rom. 8:3)

The roots of legalism are buried deep in the soil of man's sinfulness. He imagines that he can do ''the will of the Father'' through fleshly determination and self-effort, not realizing that the only one who did the will of the Father perfectly was the Son of His love, and it is only as we are surrendered to Him to live His life in us that we can do it!

True righteousness and holiness are manifestations of a life, and that life is Christ—*in Him was life, and the life was the light of men; When Christ, who is our life shall appear, then shall ye also appear with Him in glory.* (Col. 3:4)

Legalism, then, is a crude disregard of this fact: *the law of sin* can only be overcome by *the law of the Spirit of life in Christ Jesus!*

If there had been a law given which could have given life, the apostle wrote, *verily righteousness should have been by the law.* (Gal. 3:21) And since righteousness is the remedy for sin and cannot be gotten by law: *Therefore by the deeds of the law there shall no flesh be justified in His sight: for by the law is the knowledge of sin.* (Rom. 3:20) The law is not the answer to the sin problem!

Israel at Sinai traded a covenant of grace and victory for a covenant of works and defeat. May God help us not to do likewise!

1. Notes On Exodus, by C. H. M., p. 252: Pub. by Fleming H. Revell Co., New York

Chapter 3

THE PHILOSOPHY OF LEGALISM

Over one hundred years ago, C. H. MacIntosh wrote:

> "There is no evil or error more abominable in the sight of the Lord than legalism."

And yet, this philosophy has been widely accepted in the Church for centuries, though it is a perversion of the Gospel of Christ. The Apostle Paul wrote to the Galatians:

> *I marvel that ye are so soon removed from Him that called you into the grace of Christ unto another gospel: which is not another; but there be some that trouble you and would pervert the Gospel of Christ. But though we, or an angel from heaven, preach any other gospel unto you than that which we have preached unto you, let him be accursed.* (Gal. 1:6-8)

Any gospel that is not the message of the grace of Christ is under God's curse! But this 'cursed' gospel is being proclaimed with fervor around the world! It's teaching that it takes something besides the grace of Christ to save men, and keep them saved denies God's Word which says salvation is *not of works, lest any man should boast.* (Eph. 2:9) Furthermore, any doctrine that adds anything to the grace of Christ as a means of gaining, or maintaining righteousness, is legalistic, and accursed! Jesus Christ alone is the Saviour, and He saves *to the uttermost, them that come to God by Him* by faith!

Paul wrote

> *I do not frustrate the grace of God: for if righteousness come by the law, then Christ is dead in vain.* (Gal. 2:21)

It is Christ plus nothing; for if any additional merit is needed, the all-sufficient merits of Jesus Christ are nullified!

What, then, is the philosophy of legalism? It is just this: sinful, mortal man can please God by his own works of righteousness, if he will, and thereby gain and maintain divine acceptance. Perhaps the worst aspect of this reasoning is the implication: man's will is able to overcome sin; and so, we deify our will, which is rooted in self, thinking that it is the answer to our fallenness. But nothing in man can solve his problem with sin. The solution is in God, and in Him alone! This is why we need the Gospel of the grace of God with all its provisions for victorious living!

In the seventh chapter of Romans, we have the testimony of a saved man recounting his struggles with sin, and his inability to cope with it. His affirmation, *I delight in the law of God after the inward man*, is not the witness of an unregenerate nature; unsaved men simply do not delight in the law of God after the inward man! However, in spite of his heart's pleasure in holiness, he could say, *But I see another law in my members, warring against the law of my mind, and bringing me into captivity to the law of sin which is in my members.* (Rom. 7:23)

If the law of sin in Paul's members could war against the law of [his] mind and bring him into captivity to the law of sin which was in his members, then the law of sin was stronger than his human will. How, then, could he overcome the sin nature? He found the answer in a higher law! This is the declaration of his deliverance:

The law of the Spirit of life in Christ Jesus hath made me free from the law of sin and death. (Rom. 8:2)

He went on to explain

For what the law could not do, in that it was weak through the flesh, God sending His own Son in the likeness of sinful flesh, and for sin, condemned sin in the flesh, that the righteousness of the law might be fulfilled in us [not, by us !], who walk not after the flesh, but after the Spirit. (Rom. 8:3-4)

Victorious living is through Christ, and His provision made operative in us by the Holy Spirit! Furthermore, we can no more keep ourselves than save ourselves, for we *are kept by the power of God through faith unto salvation ready to be revealed in the last time.* Even though Jude exhorts us: *Keep yourselves in the love of God,* he continues with these words of praise: *Now unto Him that is able to keep you from falling, and to present you faultless before the presence of His glory with exceeding joy, To the only wise God our Saviour, be glory and majesty, dominion and power, both now and ever. Amen.* (Jude 21,24,25)

Legalism's philosophy—triumph and perseverence are results of our work—differs with Paul's words to the Philippians:

Being confident of this very thing, that He which hath begun a good work in you will perform it until the day of Jesus Christ: Even as it is meet for me to think this of you all, because I have you in my heart; inasmuch as both in my bonds, and in the defence and confirmation of the gospel, ye all are partakers of my grace. (Phil. 1:6-7)

While I believe it is possible for *brethren* to depart *from the living God,* I also believe God's elect will persevere, and their perseverence is from *God which worketh in [them] both to will and do of His good pleasure!* (Phil. 2:13)

The concept that we can satisfy a Holy God through our willpower is an erroneous theory: it is not the Gospel of the grace of God! The fallacy of urging rules righteousness as a way to holy living is shown in this passage from the book of Colossians:

> *Since you died, as it were, with Christ and this has set you free from following the world's ideas of how to be saved—by doing good annd obeying various rules—why do you keep right on following them anyway, still bound by such rules as not eating, tasting, or even touching certain foods? Such rules are mere human teachings, for food was made to be eaten and used up. These rules may seem good, for rules of this kind require strong devotion and are humiliating and hard on the body, but they have no effect when it comes to conquering a person's evil thoughts and desires. They only make him proud.* (Col. 2:20-23) (TLB)

Whenever the creeds of men add the works of righteousness which we have done to faith in Christ as being necessary to gain or maintain salvation and sanctification, they are proclaiming that Jesus's shed blood and redemptive work on the cross were not enough; our labour is needed to complete the task!

But what do the Scriptures say?

> *For Christ means the end of the struggle for righteousness-by-the-Law for everyone who believes in Him. Moses writes of righteousness-by-the-Law when he says that the man who perfectly obeys the Law shall find life in it—which is theoretically right but impossible in practice. But righteousness-by-faith says something like this: You need not say in your heart, 'Who could go up to Heaven to bring Christ down to us, or who could descend into the depths to bring Him up from the dead? For the secret is very near you, in your own heart, and in your own mouth!' It is the secret of faith...and it says, in effect, 'If you openly admit by your own mouth that Jesus is the Lord, and if you believe in your own heart that God raised Him from the dead, you will be saved.' For it is believing that makes a man righteous before God, and it is stating his belief by his own mouth that confirms his salvation...For: Whosoever shall call upon the name of the Lord shall be saved.* (Romans 10:4-13) (NTME)

Other passages—such as the following ones—should settle forever that salvation is of the Lord, beginning, middle, and end.

> *By Him all that believe are justified from all things, from which ye could not be justified by the law of Moses.* (Acts 13:39)

> *Neither is there salvation in any other; for there is none other name given under heaven among men, whereby we must be saved.* (Acts 4:2)

> *Christ Jesus...is made unto us wisdom, and righteousness, and sanctification, and redemption.* (1 Cor. 1:30)

Faith in Jesus Christ is the only way to receive salvation—and keep it!

The Word of God plainly states,

> *For by grace are ye saved through faith, and that not of yourselves: it is the gift of God: not of works lest any man should boast. For we are His workmanship, created in Christ Jesus unto good works which God hath before ordained that we should walk in them.* (Eph. 2:8-10);

And that it was

> *Not by the works of righteousness which we have done, but according to His mercy He saved us, by the washing of regeneration and the renewing of the Holy Ghost.* (Titus 3:5)

When we seek to keep by works what we have received by grace, we fall from grace and make Christ *of no effect.*

Salvation by works is impossible for men:

> *But that no man is justified by the law in the sight of God, it is evident, for the just shall live by faith. And the law is not of faith, but he that doeth them shall live in them.* (Gal. 3:11-12)

Kept by works, or legal obedience is also impossible to men, though they have been saved by the grace of God:

> *Are ye so foolish? Having begun in the Spirit, are ye now made perfect by the flesh?* (Gal. 3:3)

Or as The Living Bible paraphrases it,

> *Have you gone completely crazy? For if trying to obey Jewish laws never gave you spiritual life in the first place, why do you think that trying to obey them now will make you stronger Christians?* (Gal. 3:3) (TLB)

Salvation, sanctification, and victorious living have been purchased for us by Jesus Christ on Calvary; they are imparted by the Holy Spirit to those who repent and believe the Gospel. Law is not life; Christ is! And when we receive Who He is and what He has done for us by faith, we live!

Chapter 4

"CAST OUT THE BONDWOMAN, AND HER SON"

> *Tell me, ye that desire to be under the law, do ye not hear the law? For it is written, that Abraham had two sons, the one by a bondmaid, the other by a freewoman. But he who was of the bondwoman was born after the flesh; but he of the freewoman was by promise. Which things are an allegory: for these are the two covenants, the one from the mount Sinai, which gendereth to bondage, which is Agar [Hagar]. For this Agar is mount Sinai in Arabia, and answereth to Jerusalem which now is, and is in bondage with her children. But Jerusalem which is above is free, which is the mother of us all...now we, brethren, as Isaac was, are children of the promise. But as then he that was born after the flesh persecuted him that was born after the Spirit, even so it is now. Nevertheless what saith the Scripture? Cast out the bondwoman and her son: for the son of the bondwoman shall not be heir with the son of the freewoman.* (Gal. 4:21-30)

Many of us want to cast out the bondwoman (the law, represented by Hagar), but not her son (the flesh, typified by Ishmael). And yet, they cannot be cast out singly: they must go together. We would like to be rid of the Law, or the mocking son, but instead of casting them both out, we prefer to retain Ishmael and try to refine and improve him while rejecting his mother, the law; or, we accept Hagar and then endeavor to eradicate the flesh. If we would eliminate one, we must exclude both, for Isaac (the spiritual man) has been born in our house!

In Genesis 21:8-12, we note that Ismael's mocking was manifested after Isaac grew up and was weaned. The fleshly man always comes to the front when the spiritual man begins to grow into the stature of Christ. When this happens, we seek to make room for both: we have a difficult time of completely rejecting Hagar's son! So we tolerate, pacify, restrain, and try to change our lower nature to make it more agreeable with the new! We seem not to realize that Ishmael cannot be made better; he must be thrust out. But he is not to go alone: Hagar must leave with him. As long as she is welcomed in the household of faith, he will stay!

Do we really know who Ishmael is? Have we seen that he is a wild man, an oppressor, as well as one oppressed? Are we aware that in him there *dwelleth no good thing*? Apparently most have not, for the average Christian tries to deal with him and expects better behaviour: if he can only find a way to refine him! We might as well attempt to refine rotten hamburger. It can't be done, and God never intended that we should purify our Ishmael. He did command us to expel him. However, he and his mother have to go: *Cast out the bondwoman, and her son!*

"That is absurd" you may say. "The Law can be cast out, but not the flesh: he cannot be gotten out of the house!" In spite of our reasoning, God says both have to go!

The truth of the matter is we love Ishmael [the flesh] so much that we are unwilling to put him out! We like his antics, let him eat at our table, sleep in our bed, and romp all over the house: we just don't like the pain, guilt, and misery that come because of him. The thought of giving him up, after having him so long, is difficult to bear. We would like to be free of his mother, but let him stay! God's command and remedy for the problem is clear: *Drive off the slave girl and her son, for the slave girl's son shall never share the inheritance with the son of the free woman.* Ishmael can never partake of the rich inheritance of the Father. His gifts of grace are for Isaac, and him alone!

There's just one hitch: the wild man will not leave on his own; he must be forcibly driven out! One has to value Isaac and revere God if he is to obey. This is a difficult decision to make, but if we will believe God, and trust the Holy Spirit for His enabling power, it can be done. The joy and peace that result are wonderful blessings to enjoy. But remember, both must go!

The Law and the flesh do not belong in the believer's house. When we realize that the *old man was crucified with Him [Christ]...and has died,* and that the law has no claims on a dead man, then we can take the step Abraham did: cast them out! To our carnal reasoning, Ishmael looks alive and his mother seems to belong; but if we live by God's Word, we will walk by faith, rejecting the old life, and we will live in the power of the new!

We cannot *stand fast in the liberty wherewith Christ hath made us free* and practice wickedness: that is to keep Ishmael in the house. But the house belongs to the heir, Isaac, so that he may grow up into Christ in all things and be strengthened with might by the Spirit in the inner man so that he may *fight the good fight of faith* and *lay hold of eternal life!* Since the fleshly man and the spiritual man cannot peacefully live in the same dwelling, we need to heed God's Word: *Ye that desire to be under the Law, do ye not hear the Law...what saith the Scripture? Cast out the bondwoman and her son.*

If we haven't done so, we have not obeyed God. If we have, and they are trying to get back in, we need to *stand fast in the liberty wherewith Christ hath made us free, and be not entangled again with the yoke of bondage.* (Gal. 5:1)

Hagar, Ishmael, Sarah, and Isaac could not live happily together in Abraham's house. Harmony was impossible. Though many today would tolerate all they represent (the Law, the flesh, the covenant of grace, and the new man) in the believer's life, the living arrangement won't work! The bondwoman cannot change, and her son will not improve. There can be no peace until they are put out by faith's decision. When they are, Christ can reign, and Isaac will be blessed!

Chapter 5

SINS A LEGALIST MAY SAFELY PRACTICE (Without Disturbing His Legalism)

Of all the legalists, Saul of Tarsus, had one of the most flawless testimonies:

> *If any other man thinketh that he hath whereof he might trust in the flesh, I more: Circumcised the eighth day, of the stock of Israel, of the tribe of Benjamin, an Hebrew of the Hebrews; as touching the law, a Pharisee: concerning zeal, persecuting the church; touching the righteousness in the law, blameless.* (Phil. 3:4-6)

It could hardly have been better—*touching the righteousness in the law, blameless!* But how righteous before God was he? Though he proclaimed to the Sanhedrin,

> *Men and brethren, I have lived in all good conscience before God until this day,*

by his own admission he had been guilty of *breathing out threatenings and slaughter against the disciples of the Lord*—he who was commanded to love his neighbor as himself!

This man who excelled in his *own righteousness, which is of the law* (Phil. 3:9), also testified that he *was before [he met Christ on the Damascus road] a blasphemer...a persecutor, and injurious.* This zealot for the law *began to destroy the church and many of the saints did [he] shut up in prison...and when they were put to death, [he] gave [his] voice against them.* He was no ordinary pharisee! Punishing Christians *oft in every synagogue* and compelling *them to blaspheme...being exceedingly mad against them* had become his way of lie! Yet he was righteous in his own eyes—*blameless!* Looking back some thirty years after he first met Jesus, with a contrite and humbled heart, he acknowledged that his sins had been done *ignorantly in unbelief.*

Thank God, Saul of Tarsus had all his sins washed away in the blood of Jesus Christ never to be remembered against him! The point is: when he was under the law, he was dedicated, legally righteous, and wretchedly sinful!

This man, whom we know more familiarly as Paul, the apostle, left us a spiritual legacy of some of the most profound teaching and revelation in all of God's Word. His testimony of victorious living and devotion to Jesus Christ has few parallels in history. Consider his moving words to the Philippians [3:7-14]:

> *But what things were gain to me, those I counted loss for Christ. Yea doubtless, and I count all things but loss for the excellency of the knowledge of Christ Jesus my Lord, for whom I have suffered the loss of all things, and do count them but dung, that I may win Christ, And be found in Him, not having mine own righteousness, which is of the law, but that which is through the faith of Christ, the righteousness which is of God by faith: That I may know Him, and the power of His resurrection, and the fellowship of His sufferings, being made conformable unto His death; If by any means I might attain to the resurrection of the dead. Not as though I had already attained, either were already perfect: but I follow after if that I may apprehend that for which I am apprehended of Christ Jesus. Brethren, I count not myself to have apprehended: but this one thing I do, forgetting those things that are behind, and reaching*

forth unto those things which are before, I press toward the mark for the prize of the high calling of God in Christ Jesus.

These words ought to be the manifesto of every believer, and of the whole church!

But how did Paul gain such triumphant living? Here are his words:

> *For I am the least of the apostles, that am not meet to be called an apostle, because I persecuted the church of God. But by the grace of God I am what I am: and His grace which was bestowed upon me was not in vain; but I laboured more abundantly than they all: yet not I, but the grace of God which was with me!* (I Cor. 15:9,10)

Grace works! *For what the law could not do, in that it was weak through the flesh, God sending His own Son in the likeness of sinful flesh, and for sin condemned sin in the flesh* did! — *that the righteousness of the law might be fulfilled in us who walk not after the flesh, but after the Spirit.*

Grace not only works; it teaches us:

> *That denying ungodliness, and worldly lusts, we should live soberly, righteously, and godly in this present world.* (Titus 2:12)

Grace can be trusted!

> *Now the God of peace, that brought again from the dead our Lord Jesus, that great shepherd of the sheep, through the blood of the everlasting covenant, Make you perfect in every good work to do His will, working in you that which is well pleasing in His sight through Jesus Christ to Whom be glory for ever and ever. Amen.* (Heb. 13:20,21)

And these great works are all of grace: *not by the works of righteousness which we have done.*

Legalists can practice a righteousness which is of the Law with a bad heart. Saul did! Hatred, murder, blasphemy, injury, persecution of the children of God, and unbelief are sins a man can do and still count himself righteous.

There are numerous other sins a legalist may safely practice: stubbornness, rebellion, lust, pride, unforgiveness, and selfishness—to name a few! As long as they do not interfere with his legal conscience and are hidden in his heart, he may safely engage in them before men; but not before God! Outward appearances, however, cannot remove inward rottenness; they cannot cleanse the guilty heart of secret sins!

Make you a new heart, and a new spirit is still God's call to a religious, but lost people!

The 'safe sins' a legalist may practice, though they may be hidden from the prying eyes of men, are safe only for this time: they are damning for eternity!

Chapter 6

LEGALISTS, OR LOVE SLAVES!

It is difficult for the legalist to understand love slaves! He can hardly comprehend the thought of joyous, willing servitude. Only by being delivered from the legal mind frame can he be made to see; and this comes by the revelation of Jesus Christ. Having Him unveiled by the Spirit and comprehending what He did at Calvary breaks the chains of works dependency and sets the captive free!

Legalism is a spirit that holds men in bondage to the power of sin. To come face to face with the Divine Being as Job and Isaiah did is to have that tyranny destroyed. It is only when men see God as He is that they come to realize they are impotent to deal with sin and please Him without the grace of Christ.

But man can please God: Enoch did! And he can overcome sin. How? is the question. And the answer is by grace through faith for without faith it is impossible to please Him; *for he that cometh to God must believe that He is and that He is a rewarder of them that diligently seek Him.*

The faith-life is a victorious life: *for the just shall live by faith*; and men of faith, under the guidance of the Holy Spirit, become disciples of the Lamb—love slaves of Jesus Christ!

The apostle Paul delighted to call himself the servant (the Greek word is 'doulos') of Jesus Christ. Early Christians often referred to themselves in this manner. Thayer's Greek-English Lexicon Of The New Testament defines 'doulos' as: "a slave, bondman... one who gives himself up wholly to another's will...[one] devoted to another to the disregard of one's own interests."

What, then, is a love slave of Jesus Christ? He is a *bondman...who gives himself up wholly to [Christ's] will* and is *devoted [to Him] to the disregard of his own interests!* Such a man can be trusted, for *the righteousness of the law* will *be fulfilled* in him as he walks *after the Spirit.* Can it be imagined that he will live selfishly, immorally, proudly, and worldly—that he will practice sin? No! a thousand times no! If love fulfills the Law, and it does, then love slaves of Jesus Christ walk in holiness. The only time they fail is when they do not walk in love!

In the Old Testament, the servant who surrendered his freedom because of love for his master and others became a willing bondman for life whose motivation was not duty, fear, or money—he served because he loved! And does any man really please God if love is not his motive? Can the righteousness of the Law be fulfilled in those who walk after the flesh? No, it can only be accomplished in those who walk after the Spirit; and to walk after the Spirit is to walk in love!

Ordinary slaves live joyless, fearful, listless, duty-bound lives. A love slave lives in a different realm. His greatest delight is that he may please Him that hath chosen him to be a soldier. Since there is no fear in love, he does not live in torment; instead, he rejoices in the God of his salvation and walks by *the law of liberty,* loving his neighbor as himself!

Love slaves are free! Free from sin, guilt, law, and unacceptable service. They do not dread their master's frown, for their lives are dedicated to bringing joy to His heart. His wish is their command; His will is theirs. Nothing brings more pleasure than to hear Him say: *"well done, thou good and faithful servant: thou hast been faithful over a few things, I will make thee ruler over many things: enter thou into the joy of thy Lord."* (Mt. 25:21)

Paul, the apostle, was such a man. This was his testimony:

> *I count all things but loss for the excellency of the knowledge of Christ Jesus my Lord: for whom I have suffered the loss of all things, and do count them but dung, that I may win Christ.* (Phil. 3:8)

Serving under some of the most difficult circumstances—he had been in prisons frequently; five times he had received *forty stripes save one; thrice* he *was beaten with rods; once* he *was...stoned; thrice* he *suffered shipwreck (a night and a day he had been in the deep)* as well as various other trials, including pain, hunger, thirst, cold, nakedness, and *the care of all the churches.* Still he could rejoice in the Lord and glory in his infirmities!

Near the end of his life, he wrote a second epistle to Timothy, his son in the faith. Here are his words of triumph:

> *I have fought a good fight, I have finished the course, I have kept the faith: Henceforth there is laid up for me a crown of righteousness, which the Lord, the righteous judge, shall give me at that day; and not to me only, but unto all them also that love His appearing.* (II Tim. 4:7,8)

Only a love slave could have a record like that!

The Lord Jesus beckons us to a willing captivity (*Make me a captive, Lord, and then I shall be free!*).[1] He wants to make us His love slave. To have no law but love and to know no master but Christ is to be delivered from sin and the dominion of the Law.

When *the very spring of our actions is the love of Christ,* we walk at liberty and live in victory!

Lord Jesus, make us Thy love slaves!

Amen.

1. Song by George Matheson

Chapter 7

LIFE, NOT LAW

Holiness is life, not law! Even though the Law is holy, and the commandment holy, and just, and good, it has no power to impart life. And life is what a man dead in trespasses and sins needs. Moreover, a man separated *from the life of God through the ignorance that is in [him]* requires not a law, but that from which he is separated: the life of God!

Life cannot come from something; it can only come from Someone! *If there had been a law given which could have given life, verily righteousness should have been by the law.* Since spiritual life can only come from the Living God through His Son, by the Holy Spirit, if dead men would ever work, walk, and war against the beings of the unseen world, they must have His life! What a dead man cannot do, a living one filled with life and strength can!

And the message of the Gospel of Jesus Christ is not do and live, but look and live. The law that says, *"the man that doeth them shall live in them"* also says *"cursed is every one that continueth not in all things which are written in the book of the law to do them."* Since *all have sinned and fall short of the glory of God,* and *by the deeds of the law, there shall no flesh be justified in His sight, for by the law is the knowledge of sin.*

The Law is inflexible: *For whosoever shall keep the whole law, and yet offend in one point, he is guilty of all.* To be blessed by obedience to the Law requires perfect obedience. Ninety-nine percent is not good enough: one percent disobedience will damn the soul! *As many as are of the works of the law are under the curse* for this reason: imperfect obedience!

Holiness outflowing must come from holiness indwelling. The fountain has to be pure if its streams are to be pure! Godly living must needs have a source, and the source is *Christ in you, the hope of glory.* If the life we live in the flesh is not lived by faith in the Son of God and is not a manifestation of His life, but of ours, it is not holy no matter how good it seems!

If the Law could not give life, it could not sustain it: *Are ye so foolish, having begun in the Spirit, are ye now made perfect by the flesh?* That which could not justify, cannot sanctify: in either case, only the shed blood of Jesus can—and did! Holy living is the Holy Spirit making real in, and through us, what Jesus did on Calvary for us! This can only come through *repentance toward God, and faith toward our Lord Jesus Christ.* When this happens, the heart is purified by faith, *the love of God is shed abroad in our hearts by the Holy Ghost which is given unto us,* for we have been given a new heart!

Christianity is not mere reformation: it is a new creation: *Therefore, if any man be in Christ, he is a new creature: old things are passed away; behold all things are become new!* (II Cor. 5:17) And new men can be trusted, for *whatsoever is born of God doth not commit sin, for His seed remaineth in him, and he cannot [practice] sin, for he is born of God.*

A man with *a new heart and a new spirit* having God's laws put in his mind and written in his heart does not need external rules to help him live a holy life. When the guidance system is within, one does not need one without!

Since all other methods for godly living have failed for sinful men, and God's grace alone is the proven answer to the sin problem, why should we think of embracing them?

Is not the Law holy? Yes! But we are sinners by nature, and cannot, of ourselves, live up to it!

While many Christians may not want to admit that they still have a sinful lower fleshly nature—*In me [that is, in my flesh] there dwelleth no good thing...the law of sin...is in my members*—it is nonetheless true!

After we are saved, we are no more capable of conquering sin—in and of our natural selves—than we were before. Our determination to live by a holy law will always come short of the glory of God unless it is the result of God's working in us *to will and do of His good pleasure.* Christianity is not the consequence of our struggle; it is rather, Christ's living His life in us through faith!

Since, *in Christ Jesus, neither circumcision, nor uncircumcision availeth anything, but a new creation,* why don't we practice new creation living by the power of the Holy Spirit and see His fruit manifested through us?

If we live in the Spirit (and all Christians do), *let us also walk in the Spirit* (and all Christians may), for if we do, the righteousness of the Law will be fulfilled in us, and true holiness will characterize our lives!

God's life, not law, is the secret of godliness. May it be unveiled in us!

Chapter 8

WHAT DOES IT MEAN TO HAVE A NEW HEART?

First of all, it means to have a new center of motivation: a heart indwelt by God's love. Selfishness is no longer in control: there is a shift in the emphasis from "I" to "Christ."

The new heart, purified by faith and unworldly in its desires, yearns to give, is ready to serve, delights in God, and loves the brethren. Joyous in its faith and triumphant in its hope, it is meek and lowly, tender and true, kind and holy: it is the creation of God! Jeremiah defines it as being a place where God has written His law. Ezekiel describes it as *an heart of flesh* in contrast to a *stony heart*. The apostle Paul shows it to be the home of *the Spirit of Christ*.

When the Word of God tells of the new condition of the inner man, whether it is called *a new creature, the spirit [which] is alive,* or that which *is born of God,* it is speaking of the same thing.

A new heart does not need a long list of rules to go by; in fact, it only needs one:

> *For in Christ Jesus neither circumcision availeth anything, nor uncircumcision, but a new creature [creation]. And*

as many as walk by this rule [the new creation rule!] peace be upon them, and mercy, and on the Israel of God. (Gal. 6:15,16).

When a man has a new heart, he will live right! It is only when it becomes old, cold, and stony that it departs from holiness. When the hidden man of the heart throbs with the life of God and is permeated with His love by the power of the Holy Spirit, righteousness is its delight! *O how I love Thy law is its meditation all the day!* Hungry for truth, ready to obey, willing to listen, it is a joy to the Father. When there is within us that which longs for fellowship with Him, revels in the Saviour's love, and rejoices in the Holy Spirit, we may be said to have a new heart! For the unregenerate do not want the fellowship of God, disdain Jesus's love, and do *despite unto the Spirit of grace.*

Since *everyone that doeth righteousness is born of Him* [God], and everyone that is born of Him has a *new heart, and a new spirit,* those who practice righteousness do so because they have a new heart!

A new want to, a new allegiance, a new standard of conduct, a new direction for living is a glorious, holy, wonderful new center of being—God made it so: it is His creation! This reborn human spirit, a well flowing out in holiness, will cause godliness, faithful service, and true worship to come from our innermost being. When God's law is written in our hearts, a righteous walk will be manifested in the market place. We will be enabled to live God-glorifying lives.

This is what it means to have new hearts!

Chapter 9

CAN NEW CREATURES BE TRUSTED?

Therefore, if any man be in Christ, he is a new creature: old things are passed away; behold all things are become new. (II Cor. 5:17)

But legalists often infer (suggest) that he (the new creature) cannot be trusted unless he also has strong legal moorings for his faith. His devotion to Christ is frequently questioned if a commitment to rules of conduct is not evidenced. For such a one to rejoice in salvation by God's unmerited favor alone seems almost a heresy to some. They are afraid he may continue in sin if grace abounds.

And, yet, grace is the only effective remedy for sin! Teaching holy living, enabling acceptable service, and providing for an overcoming life, God's grace ought never be under suspicion!

It has already been proven that a sinner under law cannot be trusted, *For all have sinned and come short of the glory of God,* and *by the deeds of the law there shall no flesh be justified in His sight, for by the law is the knowledge [NOT VICTORY OVER] sin.*

In spite of the abundance of revelation truth that insists we are no longer under a schoolmaster (the Law), if we have faith in Christ, legalists keep proclaiming: saved by grace, sanctified by works!

The first century Pharisees who rose up in the council at Jerusalem *saying, that it was needful to circumcise them (Gentile believers) and to command them to keep the law of Moses* were challenged and silenced by Peter's argument that since the Gentiles had believed and received the Holy Ghost as on the day of Pentecost and had their hearts purified by faith, it was unreasonable to *tempt God, to put a yoke (the Law) upon the neck of the disciples, which neither our fathers, nor we were able to bear.*

The response of that great assembly was that *all the multitude kept silence.* I would that all the churches would do the same today that try to mix law and grace!

Can new creatures be trusted to love, live righteously, and bring glory to God? Obviously they can if Peter, James, John, Paul, Augustine, Savonarola, Luther, Wesley, and Willliam Bramwell Booth could, for all were sinners saved by the rich, undeserved grace of God! And what worked in them and in the vast multitude of redeemed saints of every tribe, tongue, and people through the ages will also work in us *that which is wellpleasing in His sight, through Jesus Christ.* While it is true that men saved by grace have sometimes failed, their failure came from yielding to the flesh and not manifesting their re-created spirit—the new man! *That which is born of God doth not commit sin: for His seed remaineth in him; and he cannot [practice] sin, because he is born of God.* (I John 3:9)

If new creatures can't be trusted, who can? Not the old nature, the flesh! It is weak, destitute of goodness, sinful, enmity against God, and unprofitable. The long history of unregenerate men proves they cannot be trusted to live righteously. Paul's estimation of the lower nature ought to be ours:

> *We are the circumcision which...have no confidence in the flesh!* (Phil. 3:3)

But new creatures can be trusted: and if they are allowed to express themselves, the outflow of their lives will be peace, joy, and victorious living.

It was of the new creatures in Thessalonica that the apostle Paul spoke in such glowing terms. He was made to remember their

> *work of faith...labour of love, and patience of hope in [the] Lord Jesus Christ.*

Further he noted their

> *having received the Word in much affliction, with joy in the Holy Ghost,*

and how they had

> *Turned from idols to serve the living and true God; And [decided] to wait for His Son from heaven, Whom He raised from the dead, even Jesus, which delivered us from the wrath to come.*

If the new creatures in Thessalonica behaved as they did, new creatures today will do likewise!

The testimony of self-righteous Saul of Tarsus should forever silence the legalistic gainsayers. Though he was blameless measured by the uprightness reached by keeping the Law, by his own admission, he was also *a blasphemer* who had *breathed out threatenings, and slaughter against the disciples of the Lord:*

But something happened that completely transformed his life: he met Jesus of Nazareth on the road to Damascus—face to face! He would never be the same. This proud Pharisee found himself humbled at the feet of his Saviour, and a love relationship with his Messiah began that was to result in a life of holiness, victorious service, and final triumph!

The disclosure to our hearts, by the Holy Spirit, of Who Jesus really is, will bring a complete spiritual change to our lives! Law can't do it, for all it can do is reveal *the exceeding sinfulness of sin.* But what the law *could not do, in that it was weak through the flesh,* Christ has done and will continue to do for those who believe.

Lest any should think we are making *the heart [which] believeth unto righteousness* to be equal to a mere mental assent to the facts of the Gospel, we would point out that Scriptural faith expresses itself in works of righteousness, and it is this believing of which we speak. As someone has said, ''Faith alone in Christ saves: but the faith that saves is not alone!''

We are not saying ''works are unimportant; they don't matter.'' We are saying ''works of righteousness are very important, but only if they are the fruit of a living faith in God!'' James, in writing about Abraham, said, *''Ye see then how that by works a man is justified, and not by faith only,''* and this is the reason: A living faith works!

Can new creatures be trusted? If a man with the love of God shed abroad in [his] heart by the Holy Ghost, having a heart purified by faith with God's laws in his mind and written in his heart, can't, who can?

But new creatures can be trusted: the old can't! By God's grace, let us live new creation living!

Chapter 10

What About Sin?

The cross of Christ is the only effective remedy for that loathsome disease called sin! Yet man would try to heal this sickness himself. His time-worn prescription, though proven futile again and again, is struggle! But his efforts always end in failure, for the simple reason that his fleshly will is not strong enough to cope with it.

Yet handle it he must, or else surrender to someone to do it for him. Jesus is willing, but as long as he [the sinner] lives after the flesh, he is unwilling! And this is the root of the legalistic problem; such a man likes to think he can control the sin nature with his self-determination. But sin, the nature, and sins: the fruit of that nature cannot be dealt with in the energies of the fleshly temperment, since they lack strength.

Legalism in the Christian is the proud, self-confident stance of one who has not yet been reduced to the helplessness of faith! Toplady, in the hymn "Rock Of Ages," so beautifully wrote:

> "Could my tears forever flow; could my zeal no respite know, These for sin could not atone: Thou must save, and

Thou alone. Nothing in my hands I bring; simply to Thy cross I cling!''

Sin cannot be remedied by self-effort; only the sacrifice of Calvary can avail, and it is available for all who truly repent and believe the Gospel.

How does the legalist handle sin? Just about every way except surrender to Jesus Christ. The following words from the Jameison, Faussett, Brown Commentary on Luke's Gospel, chapter 14, verses 28-30 are relevant:

> ''Though the contest for salvation be on our part an awfully unequal one, the human will, in the exercise of the 'faith which overcometh the world'...and nerved by power from above, which 'out of weakness makes it strong'...becomes heroical, and will come off 'more than a conqueror'. But without absolute surrender of self, the contest is hopeless.''

Surrender to the Conqueror, is the only way to conquer sin! The legalist tries to do it himself, and because he is no match for the horrid monster, he is defeated!

The *wicked and slothful servant* of Matthew 25:26 who was to be *cast into outer darkness where there shall be weeping and gnashing of teeth* failed for two reasons common to works disciples. First, he didn't really know the Lord. He said, *''I knew thee that thou art a hard man,''* but Jesus Christ, the Lord of the parable, though He is just, is not a hard man! Secondly, he was stifled by fear: *''And I was afraid and went and hid my talent in the earth.''* While grace may teach us to fear the consequences of sin,

> ''Twas grace that taught my heart to fear'' (Amazing Grace, by John Newton),

fear—i.e. slavish fear—is not a healthy motivation for a victorious life! Jesus Christ came to *deliver them who through fear of death were all their lifetime subject to bondage.* The apostle Paul wrote:

> *For God hath not given us a spirit of fear, but of power, and of love, and of a sound mind.* (II Tim. 1:7)

Fearing His name [reverencing God] is not the same as living in fear of failure and punishment. Since, love is the fulfilling of the Law, and the spirit of fear is not of God Who has given us the Spirit of love, then to claim fear is a proper means to holy conduct, is to miss His message!

Many years ago, Francois Fenelon, minister under Louis XIV of France, wrote:

> "To know God, is to love Him; therefore if we only fear Him, it is because we do not really know Him!"

And if our obedience to Him is only rooted in fear, it is not acceptable, and our works for self-justification are in vain: *For in Christ Jesus neither circumcision availeth anything, nor uncircumcision; but faith which worketh by love.* And remember, this was written in the context of the following words:

> *Christ is become of no effect unto you, whosoever of you are justified by the law: ye are fallen from grace!* (Gal. 5:4)

Martin Luther in the preface of his study on the book of Romans advised that if one does not do from the heart, the things contained in the law, he does not really keep the law—and I might add: do from a heart of love, for fear cannot fulfill the law!

While the legalist endeavors to handle sin through fear, or perhaps grudging duty or even pride—*I thank thee, that I am not as other men are*, how does a love disciple of Jesus Christ deal with it? The Scriptural answer is threefold:

1. Through faith in Christ
2. By love for God and man
3. By obedience to the Holy Spirit.

After testifying to his failure to gain victory over sin by his own strength, Paul rejoiced that

> *There is therefore now no comdemnation to them which are in Christ Jesus, For the law of the Spirit of life in Christ Jesus heath made me free from the law of sin and death.* (Rom. 8:1,2)

John, the beloved, acclaimed

> *Whatsoever is born of God overcometh the world; and this is the victory that overcometh the world, even our faith.* (I John 5:4)

These men knew that

> *By Him, all that believe are justified from all things, from which [men] could not be justified by the law* and *we are more than conquerors through Him that loved us.* (Acts 13:39; Rom. 8:37)

Faith is Jesus Christ is the way to victory over sin, for when we come to know Him, the love of God shed abroad in our hearts by the Holy Spirit will enable us to fulfill His Law. *Love worketh no ill to his neighbor; therefore love is the fulfilling of the Law.* All sin is a manifestation of our not loving God supremely and our neighbor as ourselves! On these two commandments hang all the Law and the prophets! The cure for sinning is God's love, for love *thinketh no evil...beareth all things, hopeth all things, endureth all things and never faileth.* (I Cor. 13:5,7,8)

Finally, a heart filled with faith, and love will help the believer to walk in the Spirit, and if he does, he will *not fulfill the lust of the flesh.* Being in the Spirit gives us the ability to please God; walking in the Spirit ensures our victory!

How does a love disciple face temptation and deal with sin? Joseph, the slave of Potiphar, showed us how! His answer to the enticements of his master's wife thrills my heart. His reply, *"How then can I do this great wickedness, and sin against God"* was far more sublime than "I might lose my soul" or "Your husband might find out, and kill me" or even: "It's against the Jewish religion!" No, his response to the temptress was born out of his reverence and love for Jehovah; therefore, he could say no to the flesh and bring glory to his God.

Loving obedience to the Holy Spirit, through faith in Jesus Christ, is the way to triumph over the sin problem. But the legalist does not seem to know it, for he looks to himself, instead of God. Living by fear rather than love, he walks in unbelief, carnality, and failure. He could walk in victory through the provisions of God's grace, but until he surrenders himself and his working to Christ, he cannot prevail.

Roy Hession, in his book, "We Would See Jesus" wrote:

> "Whenever a sense of sin lies upon our conscience, two

> Persons, it seems, fight to get hold of that conviction—the devil and the Holy Spirit. The devil wants to get hold of it in order to take it and us to Sinai, and there condemn us and bring us into bondage. The Holy Spirit, however, wants to take us and our sin to Calvary, there to bring us through the Door [Jesus] into peace and freedom.''

Mt. Sinai...gendereth to bondage, but the covenant of grace endorsed by the God of heaven in the blood of His only begotten Son at Calvary is a compact of freedom and victory!

The legalist would deal with his sin problem at the mount that burned with fire, but God has already dealt with it at the cross, and He longs to impart that solution to all who come to Him in repentance and faith!

O, Divine Master; Thou Who hast conquered sin, death, hell, and the grave, reign in our lives through grace by the power of the Holy Spirit unto eternal life, I pray.

Chapter 11

LEGALISTIC RELIGION

To come face to face with the Law of God and the God of the Law is an awesome experience. Israel underwent this at Sinai. Here are Moses' words recalling that encounter:

> *These words the LORD spake unto all your assembly in the mount out of the midst of the fire, of the cloud, and of the thick darkness, with a great voice: and He added no more. And He wrote them down in two tables of stone, and delivered them unto me. And it came to pass, when ye heard the voice out of the midst of the darkness (for the mountain did burn with fire) that ye came near unto me, even all the heads of your tribes, and your elders; And ye said, Behold, the LORD our God hath shewed His glory and His greatness, and we have heard His voice out of the midst of the fire: we have seen this day that God doth talk with man, and he liveth. Now therefore, why should we die? for this great fire will consume us: if we hear the voice of the LORD our God any more, we shall die. For who is there of all flesh that hath heard the voice*

of the living God speaking out of the midst of the fire, as we have, and lived? (Deut. 5:22-26)

Our God is a consuming fire the book of Hebrews tells us, and what man, whether in ancient Israel, or in our day, can stand before His blazing holiness and live—apart from mercy and grace? Even Moses, great man of God that he was, said: *"I exceedingly fear and quake."*

No one who has seen God can remain complacent in his own righteousness. When Isaiah had the vision of the 'Thrice Holy One', he was made to cry, *Woe is me, for I am undone*—or, as one version has it: *I am doomed!* (Isaiah 6:5)

No wonder the children of Israel stood afar off! Sinful men that they were, they could not "draw nigh." Only when the Lamb of God came into the world and paid for men's sins by His blood could man approach the Infinitely Holy One with confident assurance.

The awful presence of the LORD on Mt. Sinai and the revelation of His holy law nearly paralyzed the descendents of Abraham! Their terror was made plain in these words:

> *"Now therefore why should we die? for this great fire will consume us: if we hear the voice of the LORD our God any more, we shall die."*

And here was born a religion of fear: for how could a mortal man come near a Holy God, with his inabilities, and sins, and not tremble with dread? Since *there is no fear in love* and love is the basis of fellowship with God (*he that dwelleth in love dwelleth in God, and God in him)* (I John 4:16), to walk in fear is to forfeit communion with Him. Therefore, the spiritual intimacy law-bound disciples would have with the Lord is negated by their inability to draw near because of fear.

Legalism can never bring a sinful man into the embrace of the Father's love, for *as many as are of the works of the Law, are under the curse,* and those under His rejection can never enjoy the joys of His acceptance—unless, of course, the curse is removed. But, thanks be to God! *Christ hath redeemed us from the curse of the law, being made a curse for us: for it is written, Cursed is every one that hangeth on a tree: That the blessing of Abraham (justification by faith alone) might come on the Gentiles through Jesus Christ; that we might receive the promise of the Spirit through faith.*

The man who would climb Jacob's ladder to heaven by the *works of righteousness* which he has done is destined to despair for *there is none [inherently] righteous; no not one.* If the Law made nothing perfect, not because it was faulty, but because man is a sinner, then all who try to practice it as a way of life end up *under the curse.*

Many nervous breakdowns, wild fleshly excesses, and hateful, despicable, hurtful decisions have resulted from men's trying to live by the law, instead of the life which is in Christ Jesus. Legalism is a religion of failure; its adherents continue to miss the mark. Yet, in spite of the fact that they do, its advocates persist in trumpeting its cause, ladening *men with burdens grievious to be borne.* (Lk. 11:46)

"The more of the flesh we conquer, the more there seems to be to conquer." (Warren Litzman) And when one tries to subdue such a vast territory in his own strength, his defeat is assured.

When we were in the flesh, the motions of sins, which were by the law, did work in our members to bring forth fruit unto death. But now we [have been discharged] from the law, that being dead wherein we were held; that we should serve in newness of spirit, and not in the oldness of the letter. (Rom. 7:5,6) And until we are [experientially] delivered from the law and serve in newness of spirit and not in the oldness of the letter, the motions of sins, which were by the law will work in our members to bring forth fruit unto death!

Only *grace reigns through righteousness unto eternal life by Jesus Christ our Lord;* works righteousness motivated by fear and stifled by human inability has not succeeded, nor can it! The most it can produce is dead works *for all our righteousnesses are as filthy rags.* Legalistic piety, then, becomes a never-ending cycle of frustration, and futility:

> *For the good that I would I do not: but the evil which I would not, that I do. Now if I do that I would not, it is no more I that do it, but sin that dwelleth in me. I find*

then a law that, when I would do good, evil is present with me. For I delight in the law of God after the inward man: But I see another law in my members, warring against the law of my mind, and bringing me into captivity to the law of sin which is in my members. O wretched man that I am! who shall deliver me from the body of this death? (Rom. 7:19-24)

This is the testimony of an overwhelmed soul! His confession

"I delight in the law of God after the inward man,"

could hardly be one of an unregenerate man, yet his attempted lifestyle of obedience was constantly marked by failure!

What was the cause?

The commandment, which was ordained to life, I found to be unto death. For sin taking occasion by the commandment, deceived me, and by it slew me. Wherefore the law is holy...but I am carnal, sold under sin. (Rom. 7:10-12,14)

And carnal people cannot keep a holy law—saved or unsaved!

Only when The Lawkeeper, Jesus Christ, comes to live and reign in our hearts can *the righteousness of the law...be fulfilled in us.* Not until *Christ liveth in me: and the life which I now live in the flesh* is lived *by faith of [in* NAS*] the Son of God, who loved me and gave Himself for me* can I live the victorious life!

May the religion of fear, frustration, and failure be forever banished! May the "God of all grace" cause His Crucified, Risen, Ascended Son to live His life in and through us all our days to His glory!

In Jesus's Name I pray!

Amen.

Chapter 12

NEW TESTAMENT CHRISTIANITY

The Gospel of the grace of God transforms lives. The bitter are made sweet; the impure become clean; and the sad victims of Satanic tyranny are freed! This all-sufficient cure for the diseased human nature is freely bestowed on all who believe. The source of its healing power is the blood of Jesus Christ. Its curative effects are made visible in the lives of all who receive it by faith and walk in the Holy Spirit.

Since salvation is a gift given to all who believe in the name of the only begotten Son of God, works to obtain and maintain it are useless—and an insult to God. The Scriptures are clear on this matter: It is *Not by the works of righteousness which we have done, but according to His mercy He saved us;* we are saved *by grace...through faith; and that not of yourselves: it is the gift of God.*

New Testament Christianity was the demonstration of what happened in the lives of people in the first century who believed the Gospel of the grace of God! What worked then will work now, for men are the same, and so is God's solution for sin! The tremendous triumphs of those early saints over the world, the flesh, and the devil were the showing forth of Christ's life in them: they were not the results of their struggling in the flesh to keep the Law!

But the legalist scarcely thinks it possible that a man under grace, and not under the Law, could live such an overcoming life! He seems not to see that *sin shall not have dominion over you, for you are not under the Law, but under grace.* (Rom. 6:14) The grace of God that changes a man's heart and teaches him to deny ungodliness and worldly lusts is mistrusted by the legalist if it is not wedded to law!

But the grace of God—apart from the Law and men's self-righteous efforts—brings peace and produces holiness. The change that takes place in all who simply believe in the Lord Jesus Christ is miraculous!

Henry Morehouse, an English evangelist around the turn of the last century, was a preacher of grace and a passionate proclaimer of the love of God. His messages preached on John 3:16 for six or seven straight nights in Moody's church in Chicago are legendary.

One night in a little mining town in England, he spoke on his favorite theme: God's love. After the service had ended, some of the men of the church gathered around him. "Didn't you know the man that sat back there (indicating the place)?" "No," he replied, "well, that's Ike Miller, the meanest man in this country; he's pistol whipped out of town nearly every preacher that has come here. You preached the wrong sermon tonight; you should have told him about God's judgment on sinners, and how He hates sin!"

Outside, the rough, wife-beating coal miner was wending his way home. Arriving at his humble cottage, he opened the door and stood framed in the entrance. "Darling," he said (and he almost never called her that), "Jesus has sent you home a new husband. Gather the children around; we are going to have a word of prayer!" He began what he thought would be a proper way to pray: "Our heavenly Fa...ther," he began, but he couldn't seem to rightly frame his words. He tried again, but the petition appeared to fail. Then he reached back in his memory to a prayer he had learned in his childhood from his mother and began to gently plead:

"Gentle Jesus, meek and mild, pity me a little child;
Suffer my simplicity, suffer me to come to Thee!"

The message of God's love and the power of His grace had saved another wretched soul!

And the grace that saves us is the grace that keeps us: *As ye have therefore received Christ Jesus the Lord, so walk ye in Him!* For Jesus is the *author and finisher of our faith.*

If the Law cannot give life in the first place, then it cannot sustain it! We are not saved by grace, kept by obedience to the law. We are rather *kept by the power of God, through faith unto salvation ready to be revealed in the last time.*

It is not wrong to believe this; it is heresy not to!

New Testament Christianity is a manifestation of the life of Jesus Christ through the believer. Its glorious proclamation is not, "Do", but "Done!" And those who live in the power of His life *do those things that are pleasing in His sight.*

Law, since it cannot give life, lacks the ability to give victory over sin and death. Only *the Law of the Spirit of life in Christ Jesus* can do it. And this is the inheritance of every born-again child of God!

Who Christ is and what He has done is the theme of the evangelical message. What He is allowed to be to us and to do in and through us, is the measure of His redemptive reality at work in us.

A Christianity that demonstrates Christ's love, displays His life, and exults in the freedom from sin that He brings cannot be other than the genuine article portrayed in the New Testament!

Paul wrote, *for if righteousness come by the law, then Christ is dead in vain.* If the law can't bring it, the law can't maintain it. Righteousness must come by grace through faith alone.

Paul's testimony of his own transformed life was attributed to his being *called by His [God's] grace* and having His Son *revealed in him.*

The New Testament records the triumph of the grace of God in the lives of men and women who trusted Christ. No substitute can achieve its conquests; no other gospel can bring its peace! Practical in its working and dynamic in its outcome, *the Gospel of Christ...is the power of God unto salvation to every one that believeth.*

Perhaps there is no greater need in the Church than this: to have people who call themselves by the name, 'Christian', to once again experience the love and reality that is to be found in Christ. O, how we need *to know the love of Christ which passeth knowledge, that [we] might be filled with all the fulness of God.* And this is available by God's grace, through faith, to all who will receive it!

Impacting and changing the first century world was no little task. The message God used to do it was "the Gospel of the grace of God!" It will change our world, for it will change the lives of the people who live in it!

We need not fear this wondrous truth. We must, however, guard against a humanistic legalism that would try to assist or replace it!

Grace works, but works added to grace in order to earn God's graciousness nullifies the power of His undeserved favor and makes Christ of no effect—

> *Christ is become of no effect unto you, whosoever of you are justified by the law; ye are fallen from grace.* (Gal. 5:4)

Brethren, *Let us have grace whereby we may serve God acceptably with reverence and Godly fear: For our God is a consuming fire.* (Heb. 12:28,29)

Chapter 13

THE PURPOSE OF THE LAW

What then was the purpose of the Law? It was added—later on, after the promise, to disclose and expose to men their guilt—because of transgressions and [to make men more conscious of the sinfulness] of sin; and it was intended to be in effect until the Seed (the Descendent, the Heir) should come, to and concerning Whom the promise had been made. (Gal. 3:19) (Amp. N.T.)

The purpose of the Law was to reveal to sinners their sins! Once their proud, self-righteous hearts were made to feel their guilt, there was hope for repentance and the acceptance of the provision God made for them through the blood of the trespass offering.

People unaware of their disease rarely search for a physician. Likewise, men who do not see the degree of their depravity and the enormity of their rebellion against God do not seek the Saviour! The Law was given, not to make men holy, but to show them how unholy they were, in the hope they would come to the One Who can make the vilest sinner clean! Paul's cry, *"O wretched man that I am!"* came after he had really faced God's holy Law and had found himself totally unable to keep it.

The *ministration of condemnation* has achieved its purpose when the fallen sons of Adam are driven by its working from the pretense of self-righteousness, to the exposure of their guilt. O blessed ministry: for rebels against God cannot be delivered as long as they are in hiding with their sins!

So the Law unmasks sin! But can that which reveals the hideous monster be the means of salvation? Can the thermometer cure a fever, or the plumbline straighten a wall? By no means! Since victory over sin and death comes by the shed blood of Jesus and the impartation of His life, the Law which shed no blood and had no life could not bring freedom and peace.

Many Judaizers today claim that the Christian is still subject to the Law! But the Word of God plainly declares: *Sin shall not have dominion over you, for you are not under the Law, but under grace.* Further, *the Law is not made for a righteous man.* If the Law is not made for a righteous man, and the believer has been made the righteousness of God in Him [Christ], then the Law is not made for true believers.

Before faith came, we were held prisoners, locked up until faith should be revealed. (Gal. 3:23) (NIV) From this verse and others, we can see that the Law was the prosecutor, judge, and jailer! It accused the sinner, found Him guilty, and locked him up in prison to sit on death's row, condemned to die. But thanks be to God, there is a pardon readily available through faith in the Lord Jesus Christ! But we must never imagine the sheriff to be the Saviour! The *ministration of death* is not the means of life. Condemnation and righteousness are completely opposed: the Law brought the former; faith in Christ receives the latter. The Law is the way into prison; not the way out!

Proud, self-righteous men who understand their condition are fit to be saved. When they are, the Law that prepared them for salvation has finished its work!

> *Wherefore the law was our schoolmaster to bring us unto Christ, that we might be justified by faith. But after that faith has come, we are no longer under a schoolmaster.* (Gal. 3:24,25)

Urged by our guilt to seek a solution is the purpose of the

ministration of condemnation. God was not merely interested in showing fallen men their iniquity and helplessness; He wanted to induce them to ask for His help—which is Christ! Even though the stated purpose of the Law was the condemnation of the sinner, its attending hope was the anticipation that the doomed victim would seek the Saviour!

Having seen the purpose of the Law, what place does it have in the lives of born-again believers? First of all, we need to realize that *Christ is the end of the law for righteousness to every one that believeth,* and that God has written 'finished' over it for every Christian, for He has declared it [the law] *"obsolete—out of use and annulled because of age...ripe for disappearance and to be dispensed with altogether."* (Heb. 8:13) (Amp. N.T.) The Scripture is very emphatic on this matter: *the ministration of death, written and engraven in stones...the ministration of condemnation [the Law]...is done away!*

If *what things soever the Law saith, it saith to them who are under the Law,* and *we are not under the Law, but under grace,* then the Law has nothing to say to us: since it speaks only to them who are under the Law.

But here the legalists get jittery. "If the Law has nothing to say to Christians, might they not live like the devil?" They do not understand that true believers hear Someone greater than Moses speaking more glorious things than that which is done away. "*My sheep hear My voice, and I know them, and they follow Me,*" Jesus said. And once one is born a sheep and follows the Shepherd, he doesn't need road signs to tell him where to go and what to do!

When the God of heaven puts His laws in our minds and writes them in our hearts, the ones written on stones are unnecessary. may He help us to see: for people under grace and in Christ, the purpose of the Law is over.

Chapter 14

OBJECTIONS

Much of the problem in evangelical Christianity is that we have a lot of 'old men' trying to live like 'new men'! This corrupt practice leavens the Church until *pure religion...undefiled before God and the Father* is rarely portrayed. Often legalistic precepts are addressed to men with cold, backslidden hearts, who then try to measure up to what a Christian ought to be by obeying rules. But righteousness may not be attained this way. The righteousness of God which is by faith in Jesus Christ is the free gift of His grace and may not be earned.

The great fear of legalists appears to be: imputed righteousness may not result in imparted righteousness; therefore, they reason: "men saved by grace, need the law to keep them straight!"

But are we concerned that kittens may not act like kittens, or dogs like dogs, or sheep like sheep? No, they will manifest their respective natures. And will not men righteous before God, who have been given new natures, act like new men, unless hindered by the flesh, or impeded by ignorance?

The Thessalonians, who were examples to all who believed in

Macedonia and Achaia, turned from idols to serve the true and living God; and they waited for His Son from heaven! They behaved as they did because the Gospel changed their lives: they were new men!

The Corinthians walked as men because of their spiritual ignorance, and by yielding to their flesh. One writer noted: "Had they been mere men, the Apostle could not have blamed them for walking as men!"

The Gospel has not failed when new men act old; and the remedy for their conduct is not Law, *but the abundance of grace.* Those who oppose the grace message often accuse its advocates of believing that men may continue in sin that grace may abound or, perhaps even worse: they believe that receiving the grace of God without the restraint of the Law may cause men to live like the devil. A man told me recently, "If I didn't believe there were laws to go by, I would go out and get me a fifth of whiskey!"

When men want to live in sin, they need their hearts changed. While it is true, ungodly men can *change the grace of our God into a license for immorality,* born-again Christians (and is there any other kind?) overcome the world and do not practice sin.

> *No one born...of God [deliberately and knowingly] habitually practices sin for God's nature abides in him...and he cannot practice sinning because he is born...of God.* (I John 3:9) (Amp. N.T.)

The true objection to God's free and transforming grace is a wicked heart! It has no delight in such a wonderful provision for the sin problem, for in its pride, it imagines that it can do something to please a Holy God though it is sinful! Even though a man is saved, he cannot dredge out of the old nature [the flesh] obedience to God's Holy Law!

When Paul asked, *"Shall we continue in sin that grace may abound?"* He answered, *"God forbid. How shall we that are dead to sin, live any longer therein."* In his continuing argument he wrote, *Know ye not, that so many of us as were baptized into Jesus Christ were baptized unto His death? And since we have 'shared' His death, we may also through faith, 'share' His resurrection life.* (Rom. 6:4) (NAS) *"Our old self was crucified [not needs to be] with Him that our body of sin might be done away with, that we should no longer be slaves to sin: For he who has died is freed from sin.''* (Rom. 6:6,7) (NAS) This is the message of grace. It is not an excuse for sin; it is the remedy!

Another objection: ''I need Law to keep me straight'' is really saying in effect: ''the new heart cannot be trusted!'' God made the new heart; if it can't be trusted, His workmanship, created in Christ Jesus is shoddy stuff! But if anything cannot be trusted, it is the old heart, for the man that has one will not do right, for he is not right. Right people do right things, for the love of God is shed abroad in [their] hearts by the Holy Ghost!

There are those who proclaim that ''Righteous living comes by the Law!'' If it does, why didn't it work for Israel? Forty years after the compact at Sinai, Moses told them,

> *Ye have been rebellious against the LORD from the day I knew you.* (Deut. 9:24)

Thirteen hundred years later, the Prophet greater than Moses said to the Jews of His day:

> *Did not Moses give you the law, and yet none of you keepeth the law?* (John 7:19)

If the Law is the remedy for sin, why did all those under it sin and come short of the glory of God?

Since the Law does not bring righteousness, it cannot sustain it. Endeavoring to keep God's Holy precepts by the power of the mind and in the energy of the flesh has always resulted in failure. The new man will also fail if he resorts to works as the means of maintaining righteousness.

Christ is the One who produces righteousness and holy living in men. And He does it for those who live by faith—*the righteous man shall live by faith.*

Those who object to the doctrine of grace alone often claim, ''the ones who practice 'real holiness' are those who live by standards,'' and they seek to prove it by citing outward conformity as evidence.

The Word of God, however, teaches differently: *If there had been a law given which could have given life, verily righteousness should have been by the law. But the Scripture hath concluded all under sin, that the promise by faith of Jesus Christ might be given to them who believe.* (Gal. 3:21,22) The Law can't give life or sustain it. It can and does condemn all men "for all have sinned," and then because of their [and our] helplessness, it directs all to the remedy for the curse of sin: that remedy is Jesus Christ!

I do not frustrate the grace of God, Paul wrote, *for if righteousness come by the law, then Christ is dead in vain.* (Gal. 2:21) It is Christ or Law; not Christ and Law!

Rules religionists feel that regulations are needed to promote and preserve true holiness. But while the Law could pronounce the curse for the broken Law and stone the culprit to death, it could not atone for sin or sanctify the heart. Only Christ can do these things!

God has one rule for victorious living: the 'new creature rule'! What the law could not do in that it was weak through the flesh, Christ has done. Moses' Law is not the way to triumph, but the law of the Spirit of life in Christ Jesus is!

Some are afraid that grace without Law is a license to sin, but evidently Paul thought 'saved by grace' was a safe place to be, for he wrote,

> *For sin shall not have dominion over you, for ye are not under the law, but under grace.* (Rom. 6:14)

Since sin is a manifestation of not loving God supremely and our neighbor as ourselves, the thought of even considering living 'like the devil' is an evidence of not being filled with the love that fulfills the Law—it is the imagination of an old heart!

Christ's life is a saving life. It doesn't need Law to help it out!

The real objection to the Gospel of the grace of God is a wicked heart of unbelief that refuses through ignorance and willful rebellion to believe that Christ in you, the hope of glory is sufficient for victorious living.

"The life which I now live in the flesh I live by...faith in the Son of God Who loved me, and gave Himself for me" is the shout of a conqueror living a holy life!

And remember: God will work in you that which is well-pleasing in His sight through Jesus Chr· t, if you trust Him for His grace!

Chapter 15

RINGS, EARRINGS, AND THINGS!

Many years ago, a class project for Christmas brought my daughter feelings of uneasiness and guilt. Under the direction of her first grade teacher, she made a set of earrings for her mother as a gift. One of the problems she faced was she knew how I and others in our church felt about earrings: they were 'worldly'!

One afternoon, she came home from school with her special present and a troubled mind. "What would her mother think?" Dutifully she presented the gift, and when Beverly tried them on to show her appreciation, Carla immediately burst into tears! She thought her mother had sinned.

I had taught some strict standards of outward 'holiness'. Wedding rings on the fingers were acceptable: rings for the ears were not. Since I was not only her father, but the church's pastor as well, I had to be right, or so it seemed! But there were some things I did not understand. Anyway, my conscience molded hers and brought her into bondage.

Rings, earrings, and [material] things distress many when it comes to the matter of holy living. Our final authority is God.

What He says about them in His Word will guide us right. The Scriptures have quite a bit to say about these things. Please consider with me carefully some of the following passages.

First, let us look at Proverbs 25:12:

> *As an earring of gold, and an ornament of fine gold, so is a wise reprover upon an obedient ear.*

Now a wise reprover upon an obedient ear is a good thing, and so is an earring of gold and an ornament of fine gold. But the way I was taught, if a woman wore an earring of gold, it was nearly equal to an admission of a backslidden condition or, at best, a worldly heart. We often failed to judge righteous judgment, for we depended on the sight of our eyes and the hearing of our ears. Presuming to know people's hearts by outward appearances, we sometimes hurt sincere believers and grieved God.

Another passage in Genesis shows how the servant of Abraham wooed the prospective bride for his master's son by the gifts of *a golden earring of half a shekel weight and two bracelets for her hands of ten shekels weight of gold.* He was surely out of harmony with many current legalistic perspectives on 'holiness', for had he done it in our day, many would be offended when he arrayed the type of the bride of Christ.

When Jehovah recounted the covenant relationship into which He brought Jerusalem, He vividly portrayed His bringing her from the blood of her pollution to the beauty of His holiness:

> *And when I passed by thee, and saw thee polluted in thine own blood, I said unto thee when thou wast in thy blood, Live...Now when I passed by thee, and looked upon thee, behold thy time was the time of love; and I spread my skirt over thee, and covered thy nakedness: yea, I sware unto thee, and entered into a covenant with thee, saith the Lord GOD, and thou becamest mine. Then washed I thee with water; yea, I throughly washed away thy blood from thee, and I anointed thee with oil. I clothed thee also with broidered work, and shod thee with badger's skin, and I girded thee about with fine linen, and I covered thee with silk. I decked thee also with ornaments, and I put bracelets*

> *upon thy hands, and a chain on thy neck. And I put a jewel on thy forehead, and earrings in thine ears, and a beautiful crown upon thy head. Thus wast thou decked with gold and silver: and thy raiment was of fine linen, and silk, and broidered work; thou didst eat fine flour, and honey, and oil: and thou wast exceeding beautiful, and thou didst prosper into a kingdom. And thy renown went forth among the heathen for thy beauty: for it was perfect through my comeliness, which I had put upon thee, saith the Lord GOD.* (Ezek. 16:6,8-14)

Clothed with fine linen and silk wearing ornaments...bracelets...a chain on [her] neck...and a jewel on [her] forehead, and earrings in [her] ears, and a beautiful crown [on her] head, Jerusalem, the wife of Jehovah, was one who was exceeding beautiful in His estimation.

Surely the beauty God lauded in the Old Testament cannot be that which He loathes in the New! However, the things He condemned in His covenant people then, He despises in His blood-bought Church now:

> *Thou didst trust in thine own beauty, and playedst the harlot.* (Ezek. 16:15)

God hates pride and infidelity!

It is true that the passage cited is figurative. Nonetheless, God evidently did not look upon a woman adorned with ornaments, bracelets, and earrings, decked with gold and silver as obviously a wicked Jezebel. In legalistic circles, we have often assumed as much!

The point is God recognized such attire and adornment in Ezek. 16:10-13 as that which was fitting and proper for a beautiful bride.

In 'holiness churches' in our day, Christian women have been dis-fellowshipped and removed from membership rolls for less extravagant jewelry—often for wearing a gold wedding band!

Many times modern pharisees seem to be more concerned with outward conformity than with inward purity. As long as external appearances suggest holiness, the judgmental waters are unruffled. But let an infraction in visible decorum appear, and a storm of self-righteous indignation will burst upon the pews with lightning flashes of condemnation and thunderings of threatened doom!

"Overreacting" some will say. Yet there are many witnesses to the fact.

While I am not advocating an extravaganza of feminine ornamental display, I do plead for understanding among those with sensitive scruples. Let us not judge *another man's servant because to his own master he standeth or falleth.*

Rings, earrings, and material things are not the indexes of one's spirituality or the lack of it. Rather, a heart filled with love, expressing its devotion to Christ through humility and compassionate outreach to others, is the unfailing mark that identifies true Christianity!

New Testament admonitions such as this one—

> *Don't be concerned about the outward beauty that depends on jewelry, or beautiful clothes, or hair arrangements. Be beautiful inside, in your hearts, with the lasting charm of a gentle, and quiet spirit which is so precious to God. That kind of deep beauty was seen in saintly women of old who trusted God and, fitted in with their husbands' plans* (I Pet. 3:3-5) (TLB)

emphasize that God is more interested in internal goodness than external standards of holiness!

Another passage of Scripture often used in the matter of women's dress is I Timothy 2:9,10:

> *In like manner also, that women adorn themselves in modest apparel, with shamefacedness and sobriety; not with broidered [plaited] hair, or gold, or pearls, or costly array; But (which becometh women professing godliness) with good works.*

Plainly, God intends that women should adorn themselves with modest [Grk. word 'kosmios' means well-arranged, decent] apparel without the showy display of elaborate hair arrangements, expensive clothing, and jewelry. J. B. Phillips' translation says,

> *The adornment of Christian women is not a matter of elaborate coiffure, expensive clothes, or of valuable jewelry, but the living of a good life.*

To use this portion of apostolic admonition as an absolute prohibition of braiding the hair and of wearing all gold, pearls, or costly array seems inconsistent with other Scriptures that show tasteful adornment can include "gold and silver...fine linen and silk." Albert Barnes, in commenting on Paul's directives, wrote:

> "It is not to be supposed that all use of gold, or pearls, as articles of dress is here forbidden; but the idea is, that the Christian female is not to seek these as the adorning which she desires, or is not to imitate the world in these personal decorations."

A little further he commented:

> "When the heart is right: when there is true and supreme love for religion [I assume the kind spoken of in James 1:27], it is usually not difficult to regulate the subject of dress."

Are rings, earrings, and material things the bases for a person's standing in Christ? And the resounding answer is, "No!" For by faith ye stand. Why insist then, that these things are to be standards for measuring spiritual fitness?

Some claim that rings, earrings, and gold and silver things are quite worldly. But are not high-heeled shoes, perfumes, mink coats, and current styles of dress also worldly in that, in the estimation of many women on this planet, they belong to tasteful attire? Our definition of worldliness must surely include all that is in the world and that is a lot of things! While we may use cars, money, clothes, rings, earrings, and things, we must not love them, and we must be careful in their use, lest they use us!

Paul's admonition to the Romans concerning matters of conscience in the eating or not eating of meat is applicable in other areas as well: particularly of things not expressly forbidden. He counseled,

> *Let us not therefore judge one another any more: but judge this rather, that no man put a stumblingblock or occasion to fall in his brother's way. I know, and am persuaded by the Lord Jesus that there is nothing unclean of itself*

> ('nothing is intrinsically unholy' J. B. Phillips Tr.): *but to him that esteemeth anything to be unclean, to him it is unclean.* (Rom. 14:13,14)

Though his words refer to dietary matters, they can be wisely used as a principle in dealing with Christians of different persuasions as to what constitutes worldliness.

Some Christians believe it is worldly to own or drive an automobile, shave their beards—or, wear one!—wear neckties or bright colorful clothing. Others deplore wearing garments of mixed blends, such as polyester and wool, gold-framed glasses, and tapered hair-cuts! Holiness is defined by various groups in different ways: one allows wedding bands, but not earrings; some permit both; others allow neither!

Unholy wars of resentment, carnal criticism, and rejection often separate members of Christ's Body who love Him but cannot tolerate those with different modes of conduct.

Let each one have his convictions based on the best understanding of the Scriptures of which he is capable. Let every child of God walk in all the light he has. But let not any believer judge a fellow Christian as to his or her participation in Christ, solely on the basis of adornment or the use of material things!

One thing is sure: a living faith in the Christ of God is the ground of our hope of eternal life!

> "My hope is built on nothing less, than Jesus's blood and righteousness; I dare not trust the sweetest frame, but wholly lean on Jesus's name!"

Legalists make things the foundation of their hopes; New Testament Christians: Christ alone. He is our *wisdom, and righteousness, and sanctification, and redemption; He is our peace.*

Rings, earrings, and things can't damn us; the absence of them can't save us—or keep us saved; but Jesus, the Son of God can and will: *He is able to save to the uttermost them that come to God by Him, seeing He ever liveth to make intercession for them.* (Heb. 7:25)

Jesus is the Saviour, not men by their faithful adherence to legal necessities. To Him alone belongs all the power, and the honor, and the glory: Amen!

Chapter 16

HOW WE WERE BEWITCHED, AND HOW TO BE FREE!

We were "bewitched" by believing people's message, not God's! *O foolish Galatians, who hath bewitched you, that ye should not obey the truth, before whose eyes Jesus Christ hath been evidently set forth, crucified among you? This only would I learn of you, Received ye the Spirit by the works of the law, or the hearing of faith? Are ye so foolish having begun in the Spirit, are ye now made perfect by the flesh?* (Gal. 3:1-3)

Paul's teaching was clear and concise: Jesus Christ was crucified. As a result, you received the Spirit and spiritual life by faith so why do you need rules? *Have you gone completely crazy,* the Living Bible paraphrases it; *For if trying to obey Jewish laws never gave you spiritual life in the first place, why do you think that trying to obey them now will make you stronger Christians?* (Gal. 3:3) (TLB)

We, like the first century disciples, have been troubled by the 'Judaizers' who say in effect: *"You must be circumcised, and keep the law to be saved!"* To that declaration the apostles gave the reply: *"We gave no such commandment."* (Acts 15:24)

If we need anyone [even ourselves!] or anything to save us other than or besides Christ, then He is an insufficient Saviour! Christ plus baptism, footwashing, no earrings, no coffee, no golfing etc. means He is not enough. While it is true that believers should practice holy living, to add anything to His redemptive work, as a needed merit to make it succeed, is to mock Him!

As much as it seems like holiness preaching, instructions to new creatures that hint the practice of certain rules is the means to or a method of maintaining spiritual life are under God's curse. One needs the continual inflow of Christ's life to maintain vital Christianity: all other ways to achieve it are useless!

The early days of my Christian walk were marked by freedom, liberty, and victory. Then as I fellowshipped with some earnest believers, I heard one tell about his brother giving up drinking Coca Cola and how that became a testimony to an unsaved man. I thought that was a good idea, so I gave up Coke, coffee, and tea. But the Lord reproved me for my self-righteousness. He said to me one day: "You don't care who you offend and send to hell by keeping your little rules: just as long as you keep your rules!" On another occasion, the Spirit said to me: "You're trying to be more righteous than Jesus Christ Himself!"—which, of course, is impossible!

In his book, *Loving God,* Charles Colson wrote,

> "Seeing holiness as rule-keeping breeds serious problems: first it limits the scope of true Biblical holiness, which must affect every aspect of our lives. Second, even though the rules may be Biblically based, we often end up obeying rules rather than obeying God; concern with the letter of the law can cause us to lose its spirit. Third, emphasis on rule-keeping deludes us into thinking we can be holy through our efforts. But there can be no holiness apart from the work of the Holy Spirit...for it is grace that causes us to even want to be holy. And finally, our pious efforts can become ego-gratifying, as if holy living were some kind of a spiritual beauty contest. Such self-centered spirituality in turn leads to self-righteousness—the very opposite of the selflessness of true holiness." (*Loving God,*

p. 127, P2; by Charles Colson: Zondervan Pub. Corp., Grand Rapids, Michigan).

Rules holiness is never inclusive enough, and if it were, we would not be able to achieve right living by obeying its codes, for godliness is the outflow of God's life, not the fruit of legalistic obedience.

The Galatians were bewitched and turned aside from the grace of Christ unto another gospel. How did it happen? They had believed a perverted gospel that mixed Law with grace. In no uncertain terms, the apostle warned, *But though we, or an angel from heaven, preach any other gospel unto you than that which we have preached, let him be accursed.* (Gal. 1:8)

How can we be free? By following God's Word instead of the unscriptural traditions of men! Then we will *stand fast in the liberty wherewith Christ hath made [us] free.* We will be enabled to walk in obedience to the Holy Spirit. We will be given the ability to walk in love, for our faith will be in God's only begotten Son, who makes men free indeed. If love is the fulfilling of the law and we walk in love, and if we are led of the Spirit, we are not under the law, and we walk in obedience to the Holy Spirit, if those who have faith in Christ are not under the schoolmaster—the Law—and we have a living faith in Christ, then, clearly: this is how to be free!

"Come every soul by sin oppressed, there's mercy with the Lord;
And He will surely give you rest, by trusting in His Word!
Only trust Him, only trust Him; Only trust Him now!
He will save you, He will save you,
He will save you now!"

And may I add: *To the uttermost!* (Heb. 7:25)

Chapter 17

LEGALISTIC CASUALTIES

Ye did run well; who did hinder you that you should not obey the truth? (Gal. 5:7)

Many lives have been shipwrecked on the rocks of legalism that once sailed serenely and victoriously in the freedom of God's redeeming love! Trading life for law and heart-felt reality in the Spirit of Christ for man-made rules, they flounder and fall apart as the waves of temptation and sin beat against their souls. Multitudes who formerly triumphed over the world, the flesh, and the devil have settled for a dull, duty-bound religion of works that lacks *the Spirit of power and of love and of a sound mind.* Often seeking to please men by following their ideas of holiness instead of God's, they come into bondage and spiritual ruin. Believing in another gospel more than in the grace of Christ and receiving a spirit other than the Holy Spirit (the spirit of bondage leading to fear), legalists exchange the garment of praise for the spirit of heaviness.

If I attempt to build again the whole structure of justification by the Law then I do, in earnest, make myself a sinner. (Gal. 2:18)

(J. B. Phillip's Trans.) The Law doesn't make us holy; Christ does! When we undertake to be made holy by the Law, we fall from grace, and Christ is made of no effect unto us. A religion of fear (and legalism is that!) shatters conscientious souls, promotes hypocrisy, and often majors in outward performance rather than inward purity.

Casualties are everywhere: in the dead, joyless churches; in severely religious, but unloving homes; in holy-acting, poverty-stricken lives! Many works disciples try to serve a God who is always frowning; Who ever seeks to punish them for the least violation of the law. They do not really know Him as a loving heavenly Father Who loves the sinner, though He hates his sin with a perfect hatred. The fact that His Son ever liveth to make intercession for us that we might be saved to the uttermost seems somehow to be lost to them in their pursuit of legal righteousness!

Touch not, taste not, handle not does not make spiritual giants of believers; rather their growth is stunted, for rules that forbid do not minister life but death! And healthy victorious living is impossible to men as long as they are under the power of death. Rules religion, as Charles Colson has said, is not inclusive enough—some facet of 'holiness' always seems to be left out! Besides: *they [rules] have no effect when it comes to conquering a person's evil thoughts and desires. They only make him proud.* (Col. 2:23) (TLB)

Holy living is the fruit of a right relationship to God—a tree of life! And good trees bring forth good fruit, but hanging good fruit on bad trees will not make them good; and this is what legalistic, pharisaical Christianity tries to do!

Keep thy heart with all diligence, for out of it are the issues of life, [for it is the wellspring of life!] (NIV) (Prov. 4:23) Since the heart is the wellspring of life, one's doing has to be the outflow. If the fountain is sweet, loving, and holy, the waters that emanate from it will be the same! New hearts for new living is the spiritual axiom of the redeemed. All who live by this rule walk in mercy, live in peace, and glorify God.

The great tragedy of legalistic Christianity is that it leaves strewn across the landscape of time, maimed, crippled people who, *going about to establish their own righteousness, have not submitted themselves unto the righteousness of God.* Surrender is the key that unlocks the treasure of victory; struggle is not! However the strugglers become victims of the gospel of works, not realizing the Gospel of grace would set them free!

Who are these casualties in the war against sin? Their descriptions often portray us! Lives robbed of tenderness, straining in fear, stifled in the outreach of compassion by the letter of the law and the rules of men are under the hold of a tyranny worse than death!

Men bound by the chains of legalism and lacking the spontaneous love of Christ render lip-service instead of heart devotion. The "scribes and pharisees which were of Jerusalem" (who came to Jesus questioning the piety of His disciples who transgressed the tradition of the elders by not washing their hands when they ate bread) were scathingly reproved by Him when He said,

> *"Ye hypocrites, well did Esais prophesy of you, saying, This people draw near to me with their mouth, and honoureth me with their lips: but their heart is far from me. But in vain do they worship Me, teaching for doctrines the commandments of men."* (Mt. 15:7-9)

The commandments of men tend to hypocrisy and lip service! True obedience and spiritual worship is an outpouring of love that can only come from twice-born men and women of faith!

Feeble, shriveled, listless, harsh, mean, proud, and abusive discipleship is the outcome of works righteousness gained by legal means. The dying, yearning for life and the breath of God in their souls want no part of a religious system that puts unbearable yokes on their necks. In John Bunyan's immortal work, *Pilgrim's Progress,* the sight of the pilgrim running across the plain toward the wicket gate, with his fingers stopping his ears, crying, "life, life, eternal life!" is a fitting picture of all who would be disciples of the Lamb!

Christianity is life, not law. It is reality in Christ, not rules that demand deserving works. And when the captives of sin are released to the custody of the God of all grace, He gives them enabling power by His Holy Spirit to live lives pleasing to Him!

Broken, defeated, frustrated, faltering followers of "the tradition of the elders" and the Law of Moses are the 'casualties of legalism'!

The good news is *The Spirit of the Lord* has sent Christ *to heal the brokenhearted, to preach deliverance to the captives, and recovering of sight to the blind, to set at liberty them that are bruised.* And no one needs His ministry more than the legalist!

Chapter 18

VICTIMS OF DESPAIR

Going about to establish their own righteousness and not submitting themselves unto the righteousness of God makes legalists victims of despair! Falling short of the Divine perfections and intermittently trying harder to achieve them fills the works disciples with frustration and hopelessness. But God never intended His people should live thus. Purchasing victory for us at Calvary by His own blood, He calls us to "walk as children of light." Though such conduct is impossible for us in the flesh, it can be accomplished if we walk in the Spirit.

Walking in the flesh is the manifestation of our unbelief. It is only as we, by faith, lay hold of God's provision for triumphant living that we experience being *more than conquerors through Him that loved us.* As long as we, like Israel, follow after righteousness by the works of the law, *the law of righteousness* will escape our grasp. And why did they fail? *Because they sought it not by faith...they stumbled at that stumblingstone. As it is written, Behold I lay in Zion a stumblingstone and rock of offence: and whosoever believeth on Him shall not be ashamed!* Stumbling over Christ and seeking to achieve righteousness another way is disastrous. Yet, how many try to live in victory by their works instead of His strength!

The accuser of the brethren delights in condemning those who strive to attain righteousness legally! Knowing that in the energy of the flesh they cannot succeed, he prods them into working to lay hold of it by their carnal mind and will. The resultant failures of the victims of despair provide a hey-day for the enemy!

There is one great prospect for all thus ensnared: the hopelessness of their case may urge them to the Christ of Calvary, there to receive cleansing and rest. Oftentimes, God lets us go to the end of our legal rope, so we can find true holiness of heart and life through faith in Jesus alone!

How many times have conscience-smitten souls struggled with the flesh, endeavoring to crucify it, not realizing that the old man (the sinful fleshly nature) was crucified with Christ nearly 2000 years ago. God is not asking us to achieve victory over the flesh; rather, He is bidding us to receive by faith the victory already won!

Victims of despair never love enough, pray enough, give enough, and confess enough to quiet their troubled souls. Worse still, their efforts to keep the letter, often involve them in violating the spirit of the law. Tithing mint, anise, and cummin, they sometimes feel they cannot afford to give more: even if a widow needs bread, or a half-frozen wino, a coat.

But thanks be to God, there is a way out of legalistic misery, and the way is Christ:

> *Whom God hath set forth to be a propitiation through faith in His blood, to declare His righteousness for the remission of sins that are past, through the forebearance of God: To declare, I say, at this time His righteousness: that He might be just, and the justifier of him which believeth in Jesus.* (Rom. 3:25,26)

All those who have fled for a refuge to Christ have found peace and joy unspeakable and full of glory.

This doesn't mean we may continue in sin that grace may abound. It does mean, when we confess and forsake our sin with heartfelt contrition, we can find mercy and grace to help in time of need from our compassionate High Priest, the Lord Jesus Christ!

The message of grace is mercy; the demand of the law is merit! Since none deserve God's favour (*For all have sinned and come short of the glory of God* and all of mankind are *under the curse*), the only way out of our wretchedness and ruin is through faith in the Christ of God Who *hath redeemed us from the curse of the law, being made a curse for us...that the blessing of Abraham [righteousness by faith] might come on the Gentiles through Jesus Christ: That we might receive the promise of the Spirit through faith.* (Gal. 3:13,14)

There is a way out of the prison of legalism: an escape from the bondage of gloom and despair. That way is Jesus, and the key that unlocks the door is faith. Victims of despair become victors through Christ when they truly believe.

Chapter 19

WHAT ABOUT DO'S AND DON'TS?

New Testament instructions to believers are not recipes for life; they are guidelines for its expression. To those who were ''Light in the Lord'', the apostle advised: walk as the children of light. He was not saying ''walk to be''; rather he was telling them ''walk as the children of light'' because that is who you are, Light in the Lord.

In the letter to the Colossians, Paul told fellow believers:

> *For ye are dead [have died NAS], and your life is hid with Christ in God. When Christ who is our life shall appear, then shall ye also appear with Him in glory. Mortify therefore your members which are upon the earth: fornication, uncleanness, inordinate affection, evil concupiscence, and covetousness, which is idolatry.* (Col. 3:3-5)

Notice: he did not instruct them to mortify [their] members in order to maintain spiritual life. Putting to death fleshly indulgence was urged as a result of their having died, and now possessing a life...hid with Christ in God—in fact, they were told: *when Christ, who is our life shall appear, then shall ye also appear with Him in glory,*—they were going to make the Rapture! Mortify therefore was to be the lifestyle of such an exalted position in Christ.

Legalism means obeying rules to be saved and obeying rules to keep saved. It is works instead of grace. A man alive in Christ works and lives righteously not to be saved or to stay saved, but because he is saved!

The Ephesian Christians who had been blessed with all spiritual blessings in heavenly places in Christ who were accepted in the beloved and redeemed by His blood were urged to walk worthy of the vocation wherewith they were called. They were called to walk worthy of the vocation to which they were called, not to maintain their salvation, but because of who they were—blessed ...accepted, redeemed!

Having therefore these promises, dearly beloved [born-again children of God], let us cleanse ourselves from all filthiness of the flesh and spirit, perfecting holiness in the fear of God. (II Cor. 7:1) Why? In order to be? No, but because we are believers, new creatures, and temples of the Living God.

The commands of the New Testament are given to believers to be a way of life, NOT a way TO life! A man has to live before he can do, and his being alive has to come from the Giver of Life living in him by the Holy Spirit. Such a man can do holy and wondrous things, but his doing springs from being who he is because of the indwelling Christ of God!

Enjoin, instruct, correct, and discipline the true child of God all you want, if it is in the Word of God or in harmony with it; just remember: these directives do not make or keep him alive! If they are given at all, they are to be given to show him he is alive in the Spirit of Christ and to show him how he *may adorn the doctrine of God our Saviour, in all things.*

Life doesn't need law to make it live. And though the New Testament may abound with directives for living, they were given to people who live—not to make them live!

> *If ye then be risen with Christ, seek those things which are above where Christ sitteth at the right hand of God.*

Set your affections on things above, not on things on the earth. For ye are dead, and your life is hid with Christ in God. (Col. 3:1-3)

Doing flows from being, not being from doing. And a new being can live a life that will glorify God!

Your body is the temple of God...ye are bought with a price: therefore glorify God in your body and spirit, which are God's. (II Cor. 6:19,20)

The do's and don't's of the New Testament, addressed to new men, are not given to make men new, but because they are new!

Do because you are!

Chapter 20

BECAUSE I LOVE HIM!

True obedience to Christ flows from one wellspring: ''Because I love Him!'' ''If you love Me,'' Jesus said, ''you will keep My commandments.'' This motivation alone is sufficient; naught else will do. Fear is not a right impetus for holy living, for it is rooted in self, and selfishness can never be the source of godliness. Duty, too, will fail, unless it is the expression of love: for faithfulness to rules of conduct cannot, in itself, lift one into a life of purity and power. It is only when we are recipients of God's love that we can scale the heights and plumb the depths of sanctity and acceptable service.

If we truly love Jesus Christ, our greatest objective is to please Him. It no longer becomes a question of ''What must I do to maintain fellowship?'' but ''What may I do to satisfy His heart?'' All else is hay, wood, and stubble!

Those who fear loving Jesus may not be enough, who imagine that devotion to Him may result in a wandering lifestyle of sin and careless behaviour, undervalue real love! The popular notion of it a la Hollywood is not the Biblical definition! *Love [God's love in us] does not insist on its own rights or its own way. For it is not self-seeking,* it is unselfish concern for others! When this attitude inspires and captivates our lives, our service to Christ and our conduct before others will bring glory to Him!

If my behavior is conditioned on my love for Jesus (or on the lack of it)—and it surely is, then my doing is only the expression of my feeling for Him!

Stricter rules, higher standards, and legal requirements are not the need of the Church in this hour! These have never produced holiness of heart and life. Only a divine impartation of His love has and can. Where true love for Jesus reigns, the vile things of the flesh cannot. Selfishness, pride, lust, bitterness, and rebellion crouch in shame before the authority of Christ in those filled with agape love!

The servant of the Old Testament who, because he loved his master, became his life-long love slave, is the picture of every love-filled follower of the Lamb! No threats for disobedience, nor dread of the master's frown held him fast in the servitude he embraced. Love for his lord was the beat of the drum, and he marched faithfully and willingly to its rhythm. All who supremely love the Saviour will do the same!

"If we only fear Him," Francois Fenelon wrote centuries ago, "It is because we do not know Him: for to know Him is to love Him: therefore if we only fear Him, it is because we do not know Him!"

Legalists do not seem to understand that it is enough to know and love Him. They would add some safeguards and guidelines along the way to ensure purity of heart and life, not realizing that to know Him and love Him brings obedience and righteous conduct.

Show me one who is really in love with Jesus, whose spirit thrills at the mention of His name, whose heart throbs with His joy and glories in His cross, who at the same time lives a wicked, careless life.

Empty lip-service professors of Christianity may "change the grace of our God into a license for immorality" and may mock godliness with a carnal, hypocritical testimony, but love disciples, never.

‘‘Because I love Him’’ is the battle cry of the soldiers of the cross, the badge of victorious Christians, the bulwark of the believer against the floodtides of sin.

Rules to achieve holiness and regulate behavior have been annulled, and are ‘out of date’ for all who have come under the covenant of grace. A Divine Ruler has replaced them, and all who loyally love Him become *more than conquerors* through Him that loves them over all the power of the enemy!

Chapter 21

THE GOD OF SINAI AND THE HEAVENLY FATHER

The clear revelation of the Father awaited the coming of the Son! While the Old Testament contains several references to God being a father, He is more fully made known in the New Testament, where we have unfolded the message of His grace!

It's almost as if the Father was not very approachable under the Law: it was the God of Sinai who bade Israel *worship...afar off* and commanded that they should *not come nigh.* Yet, under the New Covenant, He invites us to *come boldly to the throne of grace, that we may obtain mercy, and find grace to help in time of need.* In the New Testament we are told, *In Christ Jesus ye who sometimes were far off are made nigh by the blood of Christ.* (Eph. 2:13) Who is the God of Sinai and Who is the heavenly Father? They are not two different Gods: they are one and the same!

Sinai and Calvary were contrasting ways of dealing with the sin problem. The former was a mount of justice; the latter, a place of mercy. At Sinai, wrath was promised to the offender; at Calvary, judgment for sin was poured out on the non-offender: God Himself, in the person of His Son! The legal requirement—*every transgression and every disobedience [must receive] a just recompense of reward*—has by then been traded for the Good News from Calvary: *He hath made Him to be sin for us, who knew no sin; that we might be made the righteousness of God in him.* (II Cor. 5:21) The One who did this wonderful thing is the Father, the legal God of Sinai. The stern Lawgiver is the same Divine Being that sends forth the Spirit of His Son into our hearts that we might call Him, "Abba Father." The difference being between the Judge who deals with justice, and the Father who dispenses mercy and grace! The judge who faces the criminal and the father who delights in his children may be one and the same man, yet his demeanor in each case is determined by those with whom he has to do.

At the mount that burned with the fire of His holiness, justice, and not mercy was the point of concern! Sin had to be seen in its true nature, and just punishment had to be its reward.

But the guilty sinner does not want to receive what he deserves—death! He wants what he does not deserve—life! Since by his own merits, he qualifies for the first, he must find another means to escape his just desserts—and that way is mercy!

The God of Sinai is a God of mercy, for He made provision for the erring ones through the blood of the offerings for sin. The problem under a covenant of law was this: justice had to be the recompense for sin—and justice is not mercy!

But Calvary satisfied the justice of God, for another bore our penalty! Christ's sacrifice for our sins enabled God to *be just, and the justifier of him which believeth in Jesus.* That being done, He could welcome every contrite, believing sinner into His arms of love—a forgiving Father!

Perhaps one of the greatest tragedies of legalism is that the Chief Justice of Sinai is often seen, but rarely the Loving heavenly Father!

It is hard to love a constantly frowning Deity, yet frown He must at all those who seek to be justified by law and fail!

The Gospel of the grace of Christ provides the means whereby a redeemed sinner can be invited into the Father's house to enjoy the welcome of His embrace! The New Testament believer has been called into the Father's fellowship of love, no more to serve out of fear, but out of childish delight. This is the goal of redemption: the restoration of lost children to the intimacy of the

Father's heart of love. The prodigal who returned from the far country was not only forgiven, but he was also invited to his father's table of feasting, there to enjoy the privilege of close communion!

The God of all grace bids us to know Him as the Father. No longer does He speak to us in the thunderings of Sinai; rather, He is calling from the throne of heaven where the Lamb of God who was slain from before the foundation of the world sits on His right hand, ever living to make intercession for us as a priest forever after the order of Melchizedek! The Father wants us to know, love, serve, and enjoy Him forever; living under the threatenings of Sinai will prevent our doing so.

While the Law was given to reveal *the exceeding sinfulness of sin* and to *bring us to Christ,* after we come to know Him, His mission is to show us the Father and bring us safely to His house.

Works disciples have a difficult time believing that the Father yearns to welcome them into His bosom, there to enjoy the fellowship of His love. Fear of rejection, because of the imperfections of their walk, keeps them at a distance. They do not realize that the invitation to know Him is not based on the works of righteousness which they have done, but is founded upon the offer of His mercy made possible through the shed blood of Jesus Christ, His Son!

The covenant of Sinai has been annulled, and the covenant of grace has taken its place. Under it, every believer is invited to know, not the God Who came in the thick darkness on the mountain that burned with fire, but the One Who gave His Son to die on the cross of Calvary that we might receive the Spirit of adoption and know Him as Abba Father.

> *Behold what manner of love the Father hath bestowed upon us, that we should be called the sons of God: therefore the world knoweth us not, because it knew Him not. Beloved, now are we the sons of God, and it doth not yet appear what we shall be: but we know that when He shall appear, we shall be like Him for we shall see Him as He is.* (I John 3:1,2)

The new birth makes us sons of God, the Father, and He wants us to enjoy all the benefits of that relationship in its fullness:

> *That which we have seen and heard declare we unto you, that ye also may have fellowship with us: and truly our fellowship is with the Father, and with His Son Jesus Christ.* (I John 1:3)

Amen!

Chapter 22

THE SPIRIT OF BONDAGE

For ye have not received the spirit of bondage again to fear; but ye have received the Spirit of adoption, whereby we cry Abba Father. (Rom. 8:15)

Legalism is a spirit of bondage that leads to a life of fear! And whenever slavish fear motivates our conduct, not only is the Holy Spirit not its author, the obedience that seems to come from it will ultimately fail and come short of the glory of God. The spirit of life in Christ Jesus sets us free from the law of sin and death, liberates our personalities, and enables us to walk holy before the Lord. He does not enslave us through fear, but the Devil does: the spirit of bondage is the means; devastated lives are the goal! The apostle's instruction to the Galatians to *Stand fast in the liberty wherewith Christ hath made you free, and be not entangled again with the yoke of bondage,* applies to every believer today.

It is so easy to be ensnared by a legalistic spirit ("the spirit of bondage"), and, as a result, lose our joy, peace, and victory in Christ! People bound by rules governing *meat or drink, a holy day, the new moon, or sabbath days* are certainly not standing fast in the liberty wherewith Christ made them free. Anytime manifestations of living are made the means of obtaining or maintaining the life, we may be sure something is dreadfully wrong! Let the new life flow out in *carefulness... vehement desire* and *zeal.* Let its evidences be the *work of faith and labour of love and patience of hope.* Just be careful to remember: these virtues are the fruit of a right relationship with God; they are not the root: faith in Jesus Christ is!

The spirit of bondage drives its followers to extremes and pettiness. Good and better are not enough; even the best is questionable, for by the time it is filtered through legal understanding, it will be seen to fail, and the result will be condemnation and despair. Little errors in proper conduct, possible shades of meaning in statements of fact, questions as to the purity of motivation plague Christians enslaved by legalism until the very life is drained of spiritual vitality, and the joy of the Lord is exchanged for drabness and fear.

Oftentimes, the sins a legalist tries to overcome by self-effort and fleshly restraint thrive and break out into reckless expressions of evil—completely out of control.

We would do well to remember that *the Law is the strength of sin* and *the motions of sins, which were by the Law, did work in our members to bring forth fruit unto death.* Legalism is not the remedy for sin; it is really the means by which the sinful nature is excited to act.

Paul testified: *the commandment, which was ordained to life, I found to be unto death. For sin, taking occasion by the commandment, deceived me, and by it, slew me.* (Rom. 7:10,11)

Romans 5:15 says,

> *But the fact of the matter is this: when we try to gain God's blessing and salvation by keeping His laws, we always end up under His anger, for we always fail to keep them. The only way we can keep from breaking laws is not to have any to break.* (TLB)

When God said, *For sin shall not have dominion over you: for ye are not under the Law, but under grace,* He proclaimed for us the Magna Carta of victorious living. With no laws to break, we can, by faith, experience the *grace [that reigns] through righteousness unto eternal life by Jesus Christ our Lord.* If we see grace as an excuse for sin and a license and a cover-up for an immoral life-style, we show our ignorance of the true grace of God which teaches us to deny ungodliness and worldly lusts and to live soberly, righteously, and godly in this present world.

While *all things are lawful unto me...all things are not expedient,* and I need to be careful that I...*not be brought under the power of any[thing].* My liberty in Christ must not *become a stumblingblock to them who are weak,* nor used *for a cloak of maliciousness.* And I need constantly to remember that I *have been called to liberty;* only I must not use my liberty for an occasion to the flesh, but by love I need to seek to serve others. One day, I will be *judged by the law of liberty,* Jesus Christ, Who has purchased my freedom and will then call me to give an account of how I used it.

Men who receive the grace of God in truth, who revel in Christ's life, and who understand the wonderful privileges and awesome responsibilities of such mercy are not seeking a license to sin; rather, they are striving by the power of the Holy Spirit to walk pleasing to God!

The spirit of bondage lends itself to accusations of Satan, false guilt, and slavish fear. It robs the believer of joy, stifles his faith, and weakens his witness.

While legal Christianity is sometimes preoccupied with the don'ts, the Spirit of Christ majors in the do's:

> *But put ye on the Lord Jesus Christ, and make not provision for the flesh, to fulfill the lusts thereof.* (Rom. 13:14)
>
> *Thou shalt love thy neighbor as thyself.* (Rom. 13:9)
>
> *Glorify God in your body and spirit which are God's.* (II Cor. 6:20)

Although the Holy Spirit urges the believer to *put off...anger, wrath, malice, blasphemy, filthy communication out of [his or her] mouth* and to *Lie not to one another, seeing ye have put off the old man with his evil deeds,* these are admonitions of love, not demands of slavish obligation!

When love for God and for man are the supreme passions of the heart, the power of sin is broken, and holiness prevails. Enslavement to the world, the flesh, and the devil cannot persist in such lives. Evil cannot dominate over twice-born men yielded to the Holy Spirit.

We have been called unto liberty. Freedom to live victoriously for Christ is the Manifesto of Grace. Let us, then, not be entangled again with the yoke of bondage, either as a means of justification or a method of sanctification. Let us realize that God has summoned us to life, not law!

Chapter 23

TROPHIES OF GRACE!

Ex-African slave trader John Newton was a trophy of God's grace! Dissolute, blasphemous, and rebellious, he had lived a sordid, miserable life. But one day Christ saved him! His song "Amazing Grace" is his testimony of praise that continues to echo through the centuries.

History is filled with such stories. Kings and peasants, serfs and sages, bankers and bums have acclaimed Christ's saving power. With one voice they declared God's grace sufficient.

What made their lives shine with such splendor? How did they achieve saintly character and walk pleasing to God? The answer, in each case, was always the same: *By grace...through faith.* Impulsive, hot-tempered Simon Peter, though a failure in himself, triumphed over the evilness of his flesh and became the apostle to the circumcision by grace. Mary Magdalene, Zacchaeus, and blind Bartimaeus, as well as Saul of Tarsus, Francis of Assissi, and Martin Luther overcame by grace! How did they achieve such prominent places in God's eternal purposes? Were their merits greater or their works more deserving than others? No! Could they be interviewed in heaven today, they would all say: It was *not by the works of righteousness which we have done, but according to His mercy He saved us.* Were they to be asked how Christian perfection is to be achieved, they possibly would answer:

> *The God of peace, that brought again from the dead our Lord Jesus that great shepherd of the sheep, through the blood of the everlasting covenant, [will] make you perfect in every good work to do His will, working in you that which is wellpleasing in His sight, through Jesus Christ: to Whom be glory for ever and ever. Amen.* (Heb. 13:20,21)

And it is all by grace, for *by the deeds of the law there shall no flesh be justified in His sight.*

Trophies of grace were sinners who put their trust in the Saviour; they were hopeless wretches who called on the name of the Lord! From Augustine to Billy Bray, the Cornish miner, John Huss to William Booth, Gypsy Smith to Billy Graham, the evangelist, men have ever been saved by one means: God's marvelous grace! It has always been sufficient, efficient, and necessary. Sons of Adam could not save themselves or keep their salvation by legalistic adherence to rules. God had to do it on the basis of Christ's shed blood and His redemptive work on the cross, or it would not have been done! His method has ever been, and still is, gift and not reward, and all victims of the fall are invited to partake of His gracious provision without money and without price.

Tom Kidd, the bartender from Tennessee; Socko Trenum, the heavyweight boxer from Westernport, Maryland; and Drum Stewart, the coal mine mule driver from McHenry, Kentucky had their lives changed, became preachers of the Gospel, and made heaven their home by the rich, undeserved mercy and favor of God!

His grace can be trusted, for it teaches *us that denying ungodliness and worldly lusts, we should live soberly, righteously, and godly in this present world.* It also prepares *a people for the Lord,* preserves *us to the heavenly kingdom,* and will *present [us] faultless before the presence of His glory with exceeding joy.*

You and I can be trophies of grace displayed before the universe in the realms of glory if we will but live with faith in Jesus Christ, the Savior of sinners!

Legal righteousness presents no trophies to God, crowns no brows with glory, delivers no lives from despair; but God by His grace does!

Chapter 24

UNDER LAW, GRACE!

Much to my surprise, I found that many who lived under the dispensation of the Law lived a righteousness that was not legalistic. They lived by faith, and the holiness of their lives proved it. *"O how I love Thy Law"* are not the words of a works disciple; they are the joyous exclamation of a new heart! For men were born again in Old Testament times, as well as in the New. The triumphs of Caleb, Joshua, David, Daniel, Zacharias, and Elizabeth were not gained by the Law but by the power of God's Spirit. It is foolish to think that David could have rejoiced in the God of his salvation and have described the blessedness of the man unto whom God imputeth righteousness without works, if he never experienced the reality of salvation or participated in His righteousness!

Zacharias and Elizabeth who *were both righteous before God, walking in all the commandments and ordinances of the Lord blameless,* had to be walking in the power of a divine life, for the Law could not have empowered such a performance. Even under law, multitudes of righteous people lived under grace for it was grace that provided the sin and the trespass offerings, the high priestly ministry before the blood-sprinkled mercy seat, and the water from the smitten rock.

It is a strange paradox that in the dispensation of grace, many of God's people live under the law!

Sinful men have never achieved peace with God by obeying His commandments; only His mercy in providing a blood sacrifice has made it possible! Jesus Christ, The Lamb slain from the foundation of the world, has ever been, in the mind of God, the propitiation for man's sin. Though the actual payment for the transgressions that were under the first testament was transacted at Calvary, all the lambs slain for sin under the Old Covenant were promissory notes to men of faith who accepted God's grace. Whether men looked forward to the cross or backward, the efficacy was, and is, the same!

The Paschal lamb, the smitten rock, the brazen serpent were all shadows of the substance. Just as believers partaking of the bread and wine at communion are testifying to and appropriating the merits of the atoning death of the crucified One, so the Old Testament saints—whether they believed in the seed through Whom all the families of the earth would be blessed or accepted by faith the bloody emblem of the One on the cross—were in truth receiving Jesus Christ! One of the great secrets of Zacharias' and Elizabeth's holy walk before the Lord was their acceptance of the sin and trespass offerings the God of grace and mercy had ordained!

The Law that ministered condemnation and possessed no ability to impart life could not have been the power by which diseased, broken, sinful men rose to heights of holiness and victorious living. Lest some should argue that no one under that economy did, it would be well to remember men like Joseph, Jeremiah, Hosea, and Simeon. If, *as many as are of the works of the Law are under the curse* and *by the deeds of the Law there shall no flesh be justified in His sight: for by the Law is the knowledge of sin,* then the fact that many lived godly lives under the Law shows that they prevailed in the strength of God Himself.

If *the Law was our schoolmaster to bring us to Christ* in this dispensation of grace, did it not bring men under the previous compact to Him also?

Levi, who had a covenant with God of life and peace, who

revered [Him] and stood in awe of His name, and of whom it was written, *True instruction was in his mouth, and unrighteousness was* not *found on his lips; he walked with Me in peace and uprightness, and...turned many back from iniquity,* could not have achieved his glorious testimony by that which had no life to impart! No, men under law lived under grace when they received by faith God's gracious provision for cleansing and overcoming power. The sweet singer of Israel who sang

> *Blessed are they whose iniquities are forgiven, and whose sins are covered. Blessed is the man to whom the Lord will not impute sin,* (Romans 4:7,8)

surely was a partaker of that blessedness, and if he was, it was all of grace and not by the works of the Law.

If men under law lived by grace, why can't we live by it under grace? We can, and we must.

Chapter 25

ABOVE AND BEYOND!

There is a morality higher than legalistic obedience, a greater motivation than fear, a more stringent demand than duty—and it is the love of Christ! Thinking no evil, seeking not her own, bearing and enduring all things, it exceeds all the requirements of works discipleship.

Ultimate living to the glory of God necessitates something deeper, loftier, and more encompassing than a righteousness, which is of the law. The disciplines of grace surpass the traditions of the elders and willpower adherence to rules. If we do that which was our duty to do, we are to say, ''we are unprofitable servants.'' Why? because true worshippers go above and beyond the call of duty in their service to the Master! A Pharisee may invite the Lord to dinner, but the contrite, forgiven sinner will wash His feet with her tears and wipe them with her hair. Legalists tithe mint, anise, and cummin but the love-follower of God gave *all that she had, even all her living.*

An adoring heart does not deal in minimums; it lavishes all its beneficence on the One it loves and on those for whom He died.

Caring more for satisfying the heavenly Father than pleasing men, it revels in servanthood and delights in holiness.

There is a nearness to God available to all who join the fellowship of surrendered hearts. It is elevated far above the realm of failure and fear: it is aptly described by the psalmist as "the secret place of the Most High"!

The Lord is calling us to the fellowship of His sufferings and conformity to His death for He wants us to experience *the [spiritual and moral] resurrection [that lifts us] out from among the dead [even while in the body].* The Law cannot accomplish this. But loving submission to the Christ of the cross and a day by day following in His footsteps will.

God beckoned His servant Moses to a site on the top of Mt. Sinai that He might make all His goodness pass before him, proclaim the name of the LORD, and reveal His grace and mercy. Though he took in his hand the two tables of stone, he went not to meet the Law, but the Lawgiver. There, *the LORD passed by before him, and proclaimed, The LORD, The LORD God, merciful and gracious, longsuffering, and abundant in goodness and truth, Keeping mercy for thousands, forgiving iniquity and transgression and sin, and that will by no means clear the guilty; visiting the iniquity of the fathers upon the children, and upon the children's children, unto the third and to the fourth generation.* (Ex. 34:6,7) Even under the covenant of Law, he found that the LORD God was a God of love and grace.

The God of Moses wants to take us to a similar place. He desires to show us Who He really is! Once we see Him, obedience to laws will not be nearly so important as loving, worshipping, and obeying Him!

The Lord Jesus summons us to a life of holiness that goes beyond the demands commonly understood of the Old Covenant. *Ye have heard that it was said by them of old time, Thou shalt not kill; and whosoever shall kill shall be in danger of the judgment: But I say unto you, that whosoever is angry with his brother without a cause shall be in danger of the judgment: and whosoever shall say to his brother, Raca, shall be in danger of the council: but whosoever shall say, Thou fool, shall be in danger of hell fire.* (Mt. 5:21,22)

True Christianity surpasses legalism as much as light does darkness, truth does error, and love does hatred. It cannot be successfully imitated or carnally reproduced, for it is the manifestation of the life of Jesus Christ!

A works disciple who endeavors to master the vastness of God's holiness by his struggles is like a driver of a team of oxen who attempts to cross the Atlantic in his cart. Both will drown in the process: one in the murky depths of the sea; the other, in the condemnation that comes to sinful men who try to be made perfect by the flesh.

Holy is what God has to make us before we can live holy! And the only means to such a transformation is cleansing by the blood of Jesus provided by the grace of God. This mercy is bestowed freely on all who come to the Saviour in faith. Contrary to the fears of many, the end result is holiness and abundant life. It is almost more than the legalist can comprehend.

And God invites us to this victory. It is far 'above and beyond' anything the best moralist can produce apart from grace. While it is easy to receive, it is impossible to achieve *by the works of the Law.* The simple formula for acquiring it is just this:

We which have believed do enter into rest. (Heb. 4:3)

John, the Beloved, in the last verse of the Bible, summed up the Divine intention for everyone who would be a disciple of the Lamb:

The grace of our Lord Jesus Christ be with you all. Amen.

May God grant it to every reader of these pages.

Chapter 26

THE CURE FOR LEGALISM

But may it never be that I should boast, except in the cross of our Lord Jesus Christ through which the world has been crucified to me, and I to the world. (Gal. 6:14 NAS)

The cure for legalism is the cross of Christ! Understood and appreciated, it is the answer to the many-faceted sin problem. If by it *the world has been crucified to me, and I to the world,* then *the lust of the flesh, and the lust of the eyes, and the pride of life* have met their master.

Struggling in the quicksand of self-effort, the legalist tries in vain to free himself from the demands of the Law. But the harder he tries, the lower he sinks, until rules and regulations nearly engulf him in despair! One of the favorite doctrines of the works disciples is, "You've got to crucify yourself!" Of course, none of them finally get the job done, for the crucifixion is not finally completed until the victim is dead. Those who teach this quote *"Mortify therefore your members which are upon the earth,"* and *"I die daily"* in support of it. But as study of the context of Colossians 3:5 will show, the words of verse 5 are directed to those who have died, whose lives are hidden with Christ in God. We are not told to mortify our members in order to die, but because our old self was crucified with Him, and we have been raised with Him to new life. As to Paul's statement *"I die daily"*, the previous verse clarifies its meaning: *"And why stand we in jeopardy every hour?"* (I Cor. 15:30)—i.e. *Why too do we ourselves run such risks every hour...through our union with Christ Jesus our Lord, I myself run the risk of dying every single day.* (I Cor. 15:30,31; NTLP) The apostle's encounter with the wild beasts [men] at Ephesus caused him to face dying every day. This was what he was saying—and not "I crucify myself every day".

But the principle of self-crucifixion appeals to a host of works disciples, for it puts them at the center of victorious living! Even though they flounder and fail, dedication to this belief seems somehow to encircle their lives with a halo of sanctity, causing them to glory in the flesh.

Cures that let us live with the disease are not cures at all. For the disease is deadly. For if ye live after the flesh, ye shall die, and, as strange as it may seem, we may live after the flesh in the pursuit of holiness. *Israel, which followed after the law of righteousness [did not attain] to the law of righteousness. Wherefore? Because they sought it not by faith, but as it were by the works of the law.*

Israel followed after righteousness, and to many that looks like holiness! But God said, "Israel...hath not attained to the law of righteousness." And so it is today: all the remedies for sin, including crucifying ourselves, must come to nothing if they are rooted in our flesh!

But, praise God, there is a balm in Gilead, that makes the wounded whole, and it is the cross of Christ. "For the word of the cross is to those who are perishing foolishness, but to us who are being saved (Grk. "sozo: to save, to keep safe and sound, to rescue from danger or destruction...to make well, heal, restore to health" Thayer's Lexicon), it is the power of God. The cure for man's fallenness is the cross. Alas, too many have only seen their sins taken there; they have not known that the sinner was brought there too.

> *So far as the Law is concerned, however, I am dead—killed by the Law itself—in order that I might live for God. I have been put to death with Christ on the cross, so that it is no longer I who live, but it is Christ who lives in me.* (Gal. 2:19,20; GNMM)

While it has been often said, "What you don't know, can't hurt you," (Not true: unknown poison in your food can kill you) what needs to be said is this: "What you don't know can't help you" for we can be *separated from the life of God through the ignorance* that is in us. When we see, by the eye of faith, that our sins were nailed to the cross and with them, ourselves, we live victoriously before God and men!

F. J. Huegel wrote many years ago of a man who dreamed about the crucifixion of Jesus Christ. One of the things that greatly disturbed him was seeing a hideously ugly spectacle on the cross with Him. He awoke without understanding what it was. But the memory of it troubled him. After prayer, a few days later, the Lord spoke to him: "That hideous thing you saw on the cross with Christ was you!" He, like so many of us, had not known that *our old man was crucified with Him.*

When this full revelation of the cross comes to our hearts, by the ministry of the Holy Spirit, and we receive it by faith, legalism is conquered; works discipleship is a thing of the past.

Legalism is man's effort to heal sin's cancer by other means than the cross.

> *But may it never be that I should boast, except in the cross of our Lord Jesus Christ, through which the world has been crucified to me, and I to the world.* (Gal. 6:14 NAS)

This is God's cure; it succeeds where all else fails!

EPILOGUE

Legalism isn't so much trusting obedience to laws to save us as it is living with an independent "I'll-do-it-myself" spirit when it comes to righteousness. The thought that dependent beings (and we all are) can cope with the sin problem and achieve holiness on our own is blasphemous: it simply can't be done! Anyone who imagines he can accomplish these things with his own strength is deceived. The only righteousness that is valid in God's sight is that which is perfect; and since only Christ has it, if we are to find acceptance with our Creator, we must have the righteousness of Christ!

One who constantly strives to gain or maintain right standing with God by fleshly self-effort is an offense to Him, for He can only approve that which is provided by the blood of Jesus, made real in and through us by the Holy Spirit.

Self-saving is not in the books for a redeemed people, for a 'redeemed people' of a necessity must have a Redeemer: *thou shalt call his name JESUS: for he shall save his people from their sins.* Salvation is not a self-help program; it is the glorious gift of the

Saviour, Who does the saving!

The thought of one's being able to pull himself up by his own bootstraps to gain righteousness is appealing to the carnal mind, but there is no way out of the pit unless the LORD digs us. Legalism gives the glory to man, but faith in the God of all grace gives it all to Him to Whom it belongs! If *in Him, we live and move and have our being,* then there is no life, movement, or being apart from Him—physically or spiritually. A holy being is His workmanship—not ours. We could never create such a one on our own!

Away then, with the spirit of independence and self-government in doctrine and practice. Let us never forget: it is only those who, moment by moment, rely on the finished work of Christ and submit their lives to be led by the Holy Spirit who are victorious over sin!

He is the Potter, our Maker, the Saviour, and the Author, and Finisher of our faith. We are His workmanship created in Christ Jesus unto good works. If we are, He is the Worker and we are His work. Legalism champions the ability of the pot instead of the sovereign grace of the Potter! It makes us our own saviour; and if not the author, at least the finisher of our faith.

Inherent in Paul's testimony, *nevertheless I live, yet not I, but Christ liveth in me, and the life I now live in the flesh I live by the faith of the Son of God, Who loved me, and gave Himself for me,* is the realization that holiness is not my living for God, it is Christ living in me.

Legalists think the source of right living is in themselves. Victorious Christians know that it is in Christ—all their springs are in Him.

May God help us, then, to cast off all self-reliance and to lean our whole selves on Christ, by faith, knowing that He *is able to save...to the uttermost [those who] come to God by Him.*